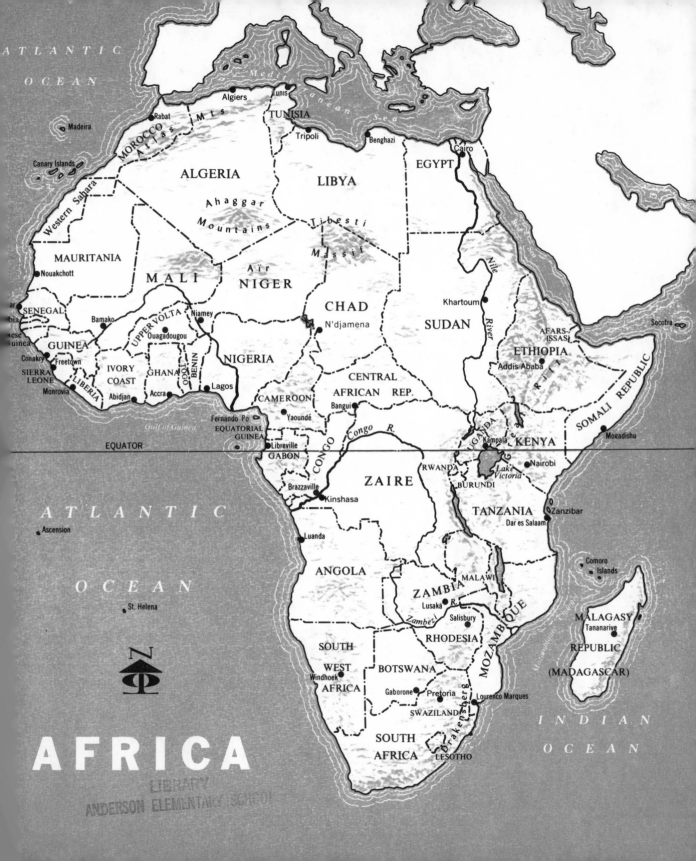

AFRICA

Enchantment of Africa

CENTRAL AFRICAN REPUBLIC

by ALLAN CARPENTER
and JANICE E. BAKER

Consulting Editor
John Rowe, Ph. D.
African Studies Faculty
Northwestern University
Evanston, Illinois

 CHILDRENS PRESS, CHICAGO

THE ENCHANTMENT OF AFRICA

Available now: Benin (Dahomey), Botswana, Burundi, Cameroon, Central African Republic, Chad, Congo (Brazzaville), Egypt, Gabon, Gambia, Ghana, Guinea, Ivory Coast, Kenya, Lesotho, Liberia, Libya, Mali, Malagasy Republic (Madagascar), Malawi, Mauritania, Morocco, Niger, Rhodesia, Rwanda, Senegal, Sierra Leone, Sudan, Swaziland, Tanzania, Togo, Tunisia, Uganda, Upper Volta, Zaïre (Congo Kinshasa), Zambia
Planned for the future: Algeria, Equatorial Guinea, Ethiopia, Nigeria, Somalia, South Africa

ACKNOWLEDGMENTS

Embassy of the United States of America, Bangui; Tourist Service, Central African Republic, Bangui; Embassy of the Central African Republic, Washington, DC; Photographs and Exhibits Section, United Nations, New York

Cover: The busy marketplace at Bangui, Allan Carpenter
Frontispiece: A Bakougni family outside their hut, Central African Republic Photographic Library

Project Editor: Joan Downing
Assistant Editor: Elizabeth Rhein
Manuscript Editor: Janis Fortman
Map Artist: Eugene Derdeyn

LIBRARY OF CONGRESS
CATALOGING IN PUBLICATION DATA

Carpenter, John Allan, 1917-
    Central African Republic.
    (Enchantment of Africa)

    SUMMARY: Introduces the history, geography, culture, government, and people of this landlocked country in central Africa.
    1. Central African Republic—Juvenile literature.
[1. Central African Republic] I. Baker, Janice E., joint author. II. Title.
DT546.3.C34   967'.41   77-668
ISBN 0-516-04556-3

4

Contents

A Folktale to Set the Scene

A SAFE ARRIVAL

One day a farmer decided to build a shelter near his fields, which were far from the village where he lived. It rained often in this part of Central Africa, and the farmer needed a place to stay dry when a sudden storm struck. The farmer gathered as many poles as he needed for the frame of the house. Because it began to get dark, the farmer decided to wait until the next day to gather the rest of the branches. So he returned to the village.

That night a lion came to the field. He, too, had been thinking about building a house. When he saw the pile of poles, he was pleased. Part of his work was already done. Happily, the lion gathered some twigs. Soon he was hungry, so he went off to hunt.

An hour later, a panther passed by. He, too, wanted a new house. When he saw the pile of poles and the pile of twigs, he rejoiced at his good fortune. The panther gathered grass for a while, then he became hungry and went off to hunt.

The next morning, the farmer returned to his field. He saw the piles of poles, twigs, and grass and was surprised to find all the building materials ready and waiting for him. The farmer quickly built the house and returned to the village to tell his friends about his good fortune.

That afternoon, a woman carrying a young child in a basket passed by the new house. She was on her way to her father's

Dancers re-enact one of the Central African Republic's many folktales.

village to visit her relatives. It began to rain, and the woman entered the house to keep her baby dry. As darkness fell, the woman and the child fell asleep in one corner of the house.

A while later, the panther came inside to rest. He curled up in another corner, without noticing the humans already in the house. Much later, the lion came inside, dragging a dead antelope. The lion ate his meal quietly and noticed neither the sleeping panther nor the woman. As the lion ate, he tossed some bones and meat into the opposite corner, the corner where the woman was sleeping. The thud of the bones on the hard dirt floor awakened the baby, who began to cry.

The lion and the panther had never heard a human cry. Both animals fled in terror, not knowing what was in the house with them. The lion and the panther spread the alarm to the other animals, and they all stayed away from the house.

At sunrise the woman woke up and found a leg of antelope meat near the child's basket. What luck, she thought, to have such good food appear miraculously during the night! She cooked the meat for herself and the child. Then she put the child on her back and safely finished the journey to her father's house.

Everyone knows that lions and panthers do not really build houses as people do. And if this tale had really been true, the animals' keen sense of smell would have told them that other creatures were with them in the house.

But the tale expresses many truths about rural life in Central Africa. Rural Central Africans feel a special closeness to the natural world, a need to share the earth's bounty with all creatures, and of course the many hazards of daily existence in the jungle and countryside. This land, called the bush, can be a fearful place for people, especially at night.

Sometimes folktales focus on good fortune that is mainly the result of chance, as this story does. In other Central African tales, it is human cunning and skill that overcome the hazards of nature. Still other tales focus on the close relationship of humans and animals and illustrate how people live within their environment.

The Face of the Land

THE HEART OF AFRICA

The Central African Republic is well named. It lies almost exactly in the middle of the African continent, about as far from Algiers on the Mediterranean Coast as from Capetown on the southern tip of Africa. It also sits midway between the Atlantic Ocean and the Red Sea. The capital city of Bangui, on the southern border of

9

the country, is about three hundred miles from the equator, and the town of Birao in the north is about three hundred miles from the Sahara.

The country has an area of 240,535 square miles. At its widest point, it measures 900 miles from east to west. Its measurements from north to south vary from 260 to 475 miles.

Five other countries share the Central African Republic's 2,700-mile border. Its longest common boundaries are with Zaïre to the south, Chad to the north, and the Sudan to the east. Other neighbors are the People's Republic of the Congo to the southwest and Cameroon to the west. Most of these boundaries are imaginary lines, but the Ubangi and M'Bomou rivers serve as the dividing line with Zaïre. A branch of the Chari River separates eastern Chad from the Central African Republic.

The Republic has no direct outlet to the sea. Its shortest route to the ocean is an overland trek of 350 miles to Douala (in Cameroon). This route is a difficult one, though. It is easier to reach the sea with a 700-mile boat trip down the Ubangi and Zaïre rivers to Brazzaville and a 300-mile railroad trip from there to Pointe Noire (both in Congo).

OUBANGUI-CHARI

During the era of French colonial rule, the Central African Republic was called Oubangui-Chari, a name taken from the country's two major rivers. These rivers have been and still are very important in the lives of Central Africans.

The Ubangi (Oubangui) River drains the southern third of the country and flows

MAP KEY

André Félix National Park, B5	Chari River, C3	Lobaye River, E2	Ouanda Djallé, C4
	Damara, D3	Logone River, C1	Ouara River, D5
Bambari, D3	Damara-Sibut Reserve, D3		Ouham River, D2
Bamingui-Bangoran National Park, C3	Dar Challa Mountains, C4	Mamberé River, E1	
Bangassou, D4		M'Baiki, E2	Saint-Floris National Park, C4
Bangui, E2	Fort Sibut, D3	M'Bali River, D2	Sangha River, E1
Bassangoa, D2		M'Bi Falls, D2	
Berberati, E1	Gordil, B4	M'Bi River, D2	Tondou Mountains, C5
Birao, B4	Gribingui River, C2	M'Bomou River, E5	
Boali, D2		Mélé, B4	
Boali Waterfall, E3	Kolongo, E2	Mobaye, E4	Ubangi River, E3
Bongo Mountains, C4	Kotto River, D4	Mount Kayagangiri, D1	
Bossembélé, D2	Kouango, D3	Mount Ngaya, C5	Vakaga River, C4
Bouar, D1	Koukourou River, D3		
Bozoum, D1		Nana River, D1	Wango, E4
Bria, D4	Lobaye-Nola Reserve, E2	N'dele, C3	
		Nola, E1	Yakotoko, D6
Carnot, D1			
		Ouaka River, D3	Zinga, E2

10

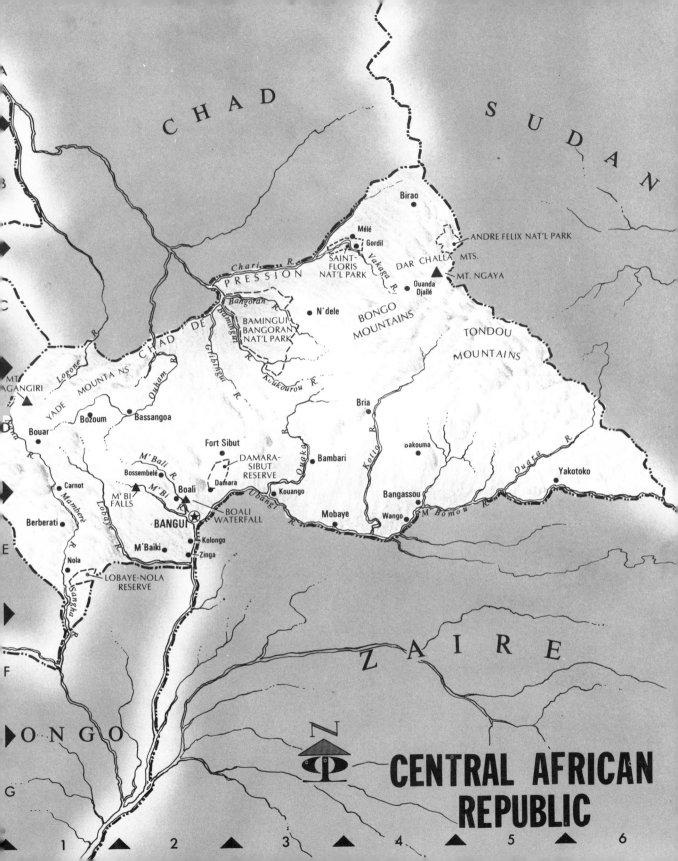

These people are paddling upstream on the Ubangi River in their dugout canoe.

into the mighty Zaïre River, which eventually reaches the Atlantic Ocean. The Chari River drains the northern section of the country and flows into Lake Chad. These two rivers link Central Africa to people in the Sahara and to others in the tropical rain forest of the Zaïre Basin.

The Ubangi River gets its name from the Boubangui, a nation of traders who have controlled the traffic on this river for centuries. The large river is formed by the joining of the Uele and M'Bomou rivers just south of the town of Ouango (Wango). The Uele rises near the Upper Nile River. It flows for 700 miles before joining the M'Bomou River to form the Ubangi. The M'Bomou River rises near the Sudan-Zaïre border and is 460 miles long.

From the point where the rivers join, the Ubangi flows in a westerly direction for 310 miles, then turns directly southward at Bangui and flows another 430 miles to the Zaïre. Near Bangui the width of the river varies from one-half mile to two miles, depending on the season. In the rainy season 33,300 cubic feet of water flow past Bangui every second. In the dry season the flow falls to only 10,000 cubic feet per second.

The Ubangi River is linked to several other rivers in the Republic. The Kotto River links it to the northeastern part of the country. In ancient days, this river system was a major route between the Darfur region of the Sudan and the Zaïre Basin.

A network of natural canals link the Ubangi River to the Sangha River in the west. The Sangha River flows almost eight hundred miles to Ouesso in the People's Republic of the Congo. Ouesso was an important market town in precolonial days. Kola nuts and ivory were traded from there up and down the Sangha River. Other important rivers in the north and west are the Lobaye River and the Logone River.

The rivers of the Central African Republic are not easily navigable. On the Ubangi River near Bangui there are dangerous rapids that cannot be traversed by boat. South of Bangui, part of the river is navigable all year. The Chari River has no rapids; therefore, it is navigable for longer distances. But its water is shallow, especially in the dry season, when some of its tributaries cease to flow.

SEMIDESERT TO RAIN FOREST

All the major types of landscape and climate of the African continent are found in the Central African Republic. North of 9 degrees latitude, the countryside is semidesert. Farther south the country becomes woodland savanna. The southernmost region of the Republic is a tropical rain forest.

The average temperature of the Central African Republic is 80 degrees Fahrenheit. In the cool season, the high temperature varies from 66 to 77 degrees. In December and January, the mean temperature in Bangui falls to 57 degrees. In the hot season, the high temperature varies throughout the country from 80 to 100 degrees. In Bangui the hottest temperatures occur in March and April, when the thermometer reaches an average of 97 degrees every day.

Most of the rain falls from July to October, although the rainfall pattern varies from place to place. April is the month of strong winds and thunderstorms. Rainfall is particularly heavy in July. The sun may not shine for days, and travel becomes difficult. By October the rainy season is nearly finished, but thunderstorms are still frequent. This is the high-water time, as the streams carry off the heavy precipitation of previous months.

The semidesert region, above 9 degrees north latitude, receives only thirty inches of rain a year, and the dry season lasts as

The hills of Zaïre can be seen in the distance across the winding Ubangi.

MICHAEL ROBERTS

long as six months—from November to April. Grasses and thorn trees grow well in the semidesert region, and cattle graze on the sparse grass.

In 1974 the severe drought conditions that devastated the Sahel of West Africa reached the Central African Republic. Livestock and crops began to suffer from lack of water. The Ubangi River reached an unusually low level, and river transportation along the Ubangi-Zaïre route had to be discontinued for several months.

South of 5 degrees north latitude, the country has an equatorial climate. In the south, there are only three dry months —December, January, and February. Rainfall stops temporarily in June and July. In this humid, wet part of the country, Bangui and Berberati receive almost seventy inches of rain a year.

Between 9 degrees and 5 degrees north latitude lies the savanna, which is less humid than the southern area. The average annual rainfall is fifty-four to six-

Because the water level was so low, ferries could not sail the Ubangi River during much of the mid-1970s drought.

Granite outcroppings are common in the north and northwest.

ty-two inches. The length of the dry season varies from three to six months—between November and April. Since many animals live in the well-watered savanna, many of the local inhabitants are hunters. The savanna also offers good farmland for growing crops.

PLATEAU AND PEAKS

The Central African Republic is a gently rolling plateau of reddish-colored laterite soils and granite peaks. Laterite plateaus cover vast surfaces in the east.

Although the Republic has few mountains, granite peaks and terraces are found in the northeast and northwest. The massifs of the northeast—Dar Challa, Tondou, and Mongo—are connected to the Darfur Massif of the Sudan. The Mongo Massif includes Mount Ngaya, which is 4,487 feet high. In the massifs of the Ouanda Djallé and Fertit Hills in the northeast, the altitude reaches 4,000 feet above sea level.

15

The Yade Massif in the northwest is a continuation of the Adamawa Highlands in Cameroon. Mount Kayagangiri which rises to 5,380 feet is part of the Yade Massif. The highest peaks in the country are in this region.

North of an imaginary line connecting the massifs of the northeast and northwest is Chad Depression. South of the line lies a sandstone plateau. Granite peaks occasionally rise out of the plain, but most of the countryside is open grassland, sloping gently southward toward the tropical forest. The lowest point in the country is near Bangui, where the elevation is only 1,340 feet above sea level.

Three Children of Central African Republic

ANNE OF BANGUI

With her parents and two brothers, Anne lives in Bangui, the capital city of the Central African Republic. She is proud of her Sango heritage.

Anne attends a school near her home, where she is in the fifth grade. Her favorite subject is literature, but she also likes science and arithmetic. Anne hopes to attend nursing school, and would like to work in the Bangui hospital.

Anne's father is a government official. He works for the Chamber of Commerce, helping tourists who come to Bangui. Anne knows that most of the tourists ask about the things that she likes to do: traveling down the Ubangi River by boat and going overland to the Boali waterfalls. Sometimes her father arranges trips for the tourists to one of the national parks or game reserves.

Anne's older brother is a skilled butcher, and he works at the local slaughter-

17

house. Her mother works at home, spending most of the day taking care of Anne's little brother. She also does the marketing, cooking, and sewing.

The neighborhood where Anne lives is near Bangui's central market. After school, Anne often meets her friends at the marketplace. Usually they buy a snack—peanuts or a fried banana—and browse through the stalls of goods. Every day, Anne stops at a certain stall, where there is a radio for sale. Anne is saving her money to buy it. She can hardly wait until she has enough money!

Anne's house is built in the European style. The interior has several rooms, and a veranda goes all the way around the house. Her father painted the outside of the house in bright colors.

Every few months, Anne and her mother travel to Anne's grandmother's home in a village on the banks of the Ubangi River. Most of the village people earn their living as fishermen or traders. Anne's mother tells her that years ago all Sango earned their living that way. Although Anne likes to visit her grandmother's village, the pace there is much too slow for her. She prefers life in the bustling city.

BARTHELEMY OF BERBERATI

Barthelemy is a twelve-year-old Baya

Left: Children relax on the steps near the Bangui marketplace. Opposite: The market's many stalls are filled with goods of all kinds.

MICHAEL ROBERTS

Left: This woman and her son stand in their village's fields. Many children like this boy and Barthelemy help their elders with the work of farming. Below: Many rural children in the Central African Republic live in homes like this one. The family's laundry is drying on the roof.

A group of men prepare their land for planting.

boy who lives near Berberati, one of the larger towns in the Central African Republic. His father is a farmer who grows millet and manioc and keeps a few chickens. Every day after school, Barthelemy helps his father in the fields.

Soon Barthelemy will be old enough to be initiated into adulthood. He is anxious for the day of the ceremony to arrive! After he is initiated, he will be given his own fields and his own house.

Barthelemy has already begun to attend village meetings with his father. The men discuss the issues concerning the village, and they talk until they agree on a decision. They also discuss the news of the day. Many people have radios, so everyone always knows the news.

Barthelemy thinks that he would like to work with other farmers in a cooperative. In a cooperative, the farmers share the work of each other's land. They also share

21

This school in Bangui is very much like Jabaku's school at Bambari.

the crops and the profits. In school Barthelemy has learned how his namesake, Barthelemy Boganda, created the first African cooperatives in the Republic.

Barthelemy's uncle is the head of the family group, called the *clan*. His uncle distributes the clan's farmland and directs the hunting. His advice to Barthelemy is to study his arithmetic, learn to read well, listen to the village elders at their meetings, and learn good farming practices from his father. Then, Barthelemy's uncle says, Barthelemy will be a strong leader of the farmers' cooperative. Barthelemy is carefully following his uncle's wise advice.

JABAKU OF BAMBARI

Jabaku's father is a merchant who trades along the old trading route from Bambari to Birao. Sometimes Jabaku goes with his father to Birao or on supply trips to Bangui and Bangassou. Jabaku loves to travel with his father, and someday he would like to travel all over Africa.

Eleven-year-old Jabaku attends a primary school near his home in Bambari. His teacher tells him that he reads and writes well. Jabaku is pleased, because he hopes someday to attend Bokassa University in Bangui. He would like to become a lawyer. On his many travels with his

Jabaku hopes to attend Bokassa University someday.

father, he has seen how important judges and the law can be.

Jabaku's older brother works for his uncle, who grows manioc and millet. Often his brother brings home manioc; then his mother prepares Jabaku's favorite dish—boiled manioc balls. Jabaku eats with his father and brother, while his mother and younger sister eat in another part of the house.

The family's house is round with a pointed roof. Jabaku's father and brother built the house and painted it themselves. They used vegetable juices to make the paint. The whole house is decorated with painted scenes. Jabaku's favorite is a hunting scene on the front of the house.

Next year Jabaku will move from this house. He will live with boys his own age in a separate place. Elders of the clan will teach the boys about their people's history and religious beliefs, and about the boys' duties toward society. The boys will wear special clothes, eat special foods, and be initiated into adulthood. Jabaku is very excited about becoming a man! In the meantime, he studies hard and enjoys his travels.

Central African Republic Yesterday

EARLY INHABITANTS

Little is known about the ancient history of the Central African Republic, although many prehistoric remains have been found. In the Neolithic period, the area that is now the Republic was a passageway between two great swamps—all that remained of what had once been two large, inland seas. The seas were in the areas of lower Chad and the Sangha-Ubangi-Zaïre rivers.

Sources of information about early peoples in the Central African Republic are sparse. Archaeology provides some knowledge, as do studies of various language groups and their origins. Other sources of information for more recent times include history told orally through the generations and written documents of other countries. None of the peoples in the Central African Republic had a written language.

From archaeological findings, it is known that early peoples lived by hunting and gathering. In the savanna regions of Central Africa, people learned to plant and harvest cereal grains and to domesticate animals. To live in the forest, people had to cultivate the tuber (root) crops be-

Traditional dress and hairstyles in the Central African Republic are shown in these wooden figures.

Pottery has been made in the Central African Republic for centuries.

cause grains do not grow well in the forests. Cattle could not live there because of the deadly tsetse fly. Some anthropologists believe that early people must have known how to make iron before they could live in the tropical rain forest. Other experts say that knowledge of metals came later.

Archaeologists have discovered some artifacts of early peoples, including tools, household utensils, food, and jewelry. Ivory ornaments, stone tools, and pottery are common relics of the past civilizations in Central Africa. Bifacial handaxes (axes with both ends the same) have been found along the M'Bali River.

Oral traditions explain what people believe happened in the more recent past. These traditions stress what is most important to the people. For example, citizens of a highly centralized state consider the genealogy (family history) of their ruler's family as significant. An official court historian studies the family's past and recites it during certain ceremonies. In Africa, court genealogies often link the living ruler to the legendary hero of his or her ethnic group. Events of the past are presented so as to bring honor to the current leader. In less-structured societies, on the other hand, the genealogy of the ruler is of little importance. The ruler's ancestry may be known only to the third generation (the grandparents). Oral traditions of most of the ethnic groups in Central Africa concentrate only on the recent past.

References to Central Africa appear in the writings of other peoples. The Greeks and the Romans knew about the Ubangi River because some of their slaves had come from there. They called the river "the Nile of the Blacks." A few inscriptions on Egyptian monuments mention the area of Central Africa. The Egyptians knew about the pygmies, whom they

Children begin to learn the dances and other traditions of their people when they are very young.

called dwarfs. The pygmies are one of the Republic's two ethnic groups who inhabited the region in ancient times. The other group was probably made up of peoples now known as "guinea-neolithic." They did not yet know how to make iron tools. Nevertheless, their polished stone axes and hoes permitted them to live on the edge of the forest zone and even to begin to penetrate it.

BANTU MIGRATIONS

Thousands of years ago, Bantu-speaking people from Nigeria and Cameroon began to migrate east and south in small groups. Within a few hundred years, Bantu speakers had spread over most of Central Africa.

As the centuries passed, the scattered groups of Bantu speakers mixed with other peoples, and the basic language began to change. The changes were different for each group. Today the descendants of the Bantu speakers speak many languages and are spread across Africa from Douala (in Cameroon) to the Indian Ocean and as far south as South Africa. Linguists are studying their languages for clues to the migrations and events of the past.

Early Bantu migrants in the Central African Republic seem to have spread two ways: overland among the "guinea-neolithic" agriculturalists, and down rivers in canoes as fishermen. Both settled in small, independent communities. They were governed by elders, who represented their ancestors. Custom, public opinion, and kinship ties held the groups together. Most of the people hunted, fished, or farmed. Some specialized in crafts or construction. Unlike earlier settlers, the Bantu-speakers are thought to have had knowledge of ironworking, which gave them a decided advantage over previous inhabitants. Since tools and weapons were essential to life, blacksmiths were very important. In fact, they were believed to possess supernatural powers, and their forges were sacred to their villages. The blacksmith made knives, hoes, axes, spears, and arrows. He took part in the initiation service for boys. Sometimes he was the community's religious diviner or even its judge.

The Bantu of Central Africa maintained contact with other societies. By the sixteenth century, they were part of an important trade network that linked Islamic societies of the north to the non-Islamic socities of the Zaïre forest. Caravans came from the Muslim kingdom of Bornu (in what is now Nigeria) and from the Darfur (in present-day Sudan) to trade with the mighty kingdom of Kongo (in what is now part of Zaïre and Angola). The river people living along the Ubangi and Zaïre rivers controlled the flow of trade.

Portuguese traders on the Atlantic coast

Opposite top: Men in many of the Central African Republic's ethnic groups traditionally have the tasks of fighting, hunting, and fishing. Opposite bottom: The Central African Republic's earliest people did not know the modern techniques used on this farm.

Muslims operate this market near Bangui.

heard of these river tradesmen and wrote about them. The Portuguese introduced a new crop—corn—from South America, and it spread into Central Africa along the river trade routes.

MUSLIM RAIDS AND GREAT MIGRATIONS

By the seventeenth century, the Muslim kingdoms to the far north began to look upon Central Africa as a source for slaves. The Muslims established Kouka near Lake Chad as a great slave market. For some of these Muslim communities, slave-trading was basic to their economy.

Slave raids reached as far south as the Ubangi River. These raids disrupted the populations of the Ubangi, Lobaye, and Sangha valleys. Some Central Africans fought the invaders; others fled to the massifs or into the forest. Some groups changed their locations so often that they spent most of their time wandering around, as seminomads do. During this era, much of the history and oral traditions of the Republic's peoples were lost forever. Slaves captured in what is now the Central African Republic were sold in the markets of Egypt, North Africa, Zanzibar, Brazil, and the West Indies.

The raids for slaves caused several ethnic migrations in the eighteenth century

This mosque, *or place of worship for Muslims, is just one of the many scattered through the* Central African Republic.

and a large-scale migration of peoples in the nineteenth century. Among the first groups to migrate were the Zande, who originally lived southeast of Lake Chad on the sources of the Chari River. They moved south and then east to the Uele River source (south of the present-day town of Wango) by 1800. Led by a man named Ngura, they organized their own empire. Royal clans under Ngura's sons set up their own kingdoms and appointed governors over subdivisions of the kingdoms. All clans paid tribute to the clan head. All males were subject to military duty. The Zande were strong enough to defeat and then negotiate with the Arab slave raiders, and they eventually became slave traders themselves.

Wars between the Muslim kingdoms of Bornu in northern Nigeria and peoples south of them disturbed the Baya people of Cameroon. This caused a second great migration. The Baya moved east toward the Chari Valley and settled in the Haute-Sangha and Lobaye regions of the Republic. But even there, slave raiders threatened their villages. Sometime after 1820, the Baya (or Mandjia, as they called themselves) moved into the Bangui region, pushing out or absorbing the native peoples. Some of the Baya settled in Zaïre, then returned to Central Africa. The original river peoples continued to control traffic on the Ubangi River.

The original homeland of a third great migrating group—the Banda—was the area just west of Darfur (Sudan). Around 1830, pressed hard by devastating slave raids, the Banda migrated in several directions. War leaders led small groups south in stages. Some Banda moved into the central region of the Republic, while others went south to Bambari and the Ubangi River. Still other groups settled near the place where the Kotto and Ubangi rivers join. In less than half a century, the Banda had migrated more than nine hundred miles.

The forest area of the southwest and the Ubangi River valley became the final home for other peoples who had been disturbed by the great migrations, such as the M'Baka, Lissongo, Pande, and M'Bimou. The pygmies, original inhabitants of the southwest, moved far into the rain forest to avoid the newcomers.

MUSLIM PRINCES

Slave raids continued to threaten Central Africans until 1900. Muslim raiders divided Central Africa into zones, one for each sultan to the north and east of the present-day Republic. The traders called Central Africa "rich in men." The common practice of raiding parties was to seize all persons young enough to become slaves and to slaughter the old and ill.

The Muslim merchant-princes of the Upper Nile became powerful and wealthy. One such man, Zubayr Pasha, dominated the Bahr al Ghazal region of the southern Sudan by 1870. Within a few years, he had conquered Darfur. His fortified trading posts spread along the Nile and Ubangi rivers, and his soldiers raided for slaves as far south as the place where the Kotto and Ubangi rivers join. The Zande people of Central Africa supplied him with slaves captured from their enemies. The increasing independence of Zubayr Pasha angered his sovereign, the khedive of Egypt. Zubayr Pasha was recalled to Cairo, arrested, and imprisoned.

RABAH

Zubayr Pasha's lieutenant, Rabah Zubayr, organized a band of loyal followers. Because his mother was a Mandjia, he was able to recruit soldiers even among the peoples of the Central African Republic. In 1884 Rabah captured land including much of what is now the northern Central African Republic and made his capital at N'Dele. Then he moved his forces northwest out of the Central African area. He destroyed Kouka on Lake Chad and built a new capital nearby in 1893. In the same year, Rabah captured the ancient empire of Bornu in northern Nigeria.

Many of the forests where people retreated from invaders have become very depleted. The government has taken control of them to try to restore them to their original splendor. This forest, called La Grande Forêt *(The Great Forest) is between Bangui and M'Baiki.*

For a few more years, Rabah ruled a vast empire. To maintain his empire Rabah needed guns. He could get guns from Egypt only in exchange for slaves. So the slave trade flourished under Rabah. Rabah remained a powerful ruler in Central Africa until he was killed by the French on April 22, 1900.

THE FRENCH

Arabs were not the only foreigners who dreamed of a Central African empire. Europeans, too, were eager to stake claims to new territory in Africa. After 1850 explorers traveled up the Nile in search of new lands and peoples. In the 1870s, King Leopold II of Belgium declared his intention of setting up a series of scientific posts in Central Africa and coordinating the efforts of all European explorers. His real purpose was to stake territorial claims

for himself. Leopold hired Henry Morton Stanley to help him. In 1877 Stanley had an unpromising encounter with the Boubangui near the mouth of the Ubangi River. Nonetheless, he went on to complete a road from the Lower Congo (Zaïre) River to Malebo (Stanley) Pool (at present-day Brazzaville) by 1884. He launched steamers on the Upper Congo River, where he built trading stations.

In 1880 Pierre Savorgnan de Brazza, a Frenchman, reached Malebo Pool via Gabon. He made an agreement with the Boubangui and other river people. Like Stanley, de Brazza brought trade goods to Malebo Pool, but he did not try to handle negotiations himself, as Stanley did. De Brazza left the trading in the hands of the local merchants. In 1886 de Brazza became commissioner general of the French Congo, a post he held for eleven years.

THE FOUNDING OF BANGUI

The French were competing with King Leopold of the Belgians to lay claim to

Opposite top: The shores of Zaïre as seen from Bangui. Belgium and France quarreled over this part of Africa. Belgium won control of Zaïre. The Central African Republic went to France. Opposite bottom: The French founded Bangui in 1889. Below: As the signs at this soccer stadium show, the French language is the one spoken by most of the people.

Villages throughout the Central African Republic looked like this one in the days when the Europeans were first arriving—and many still look this way today.

West African territories. The French soon realized the need for a post on the Ubangi River. It would serve as a jumping-off place to launch their expeditions north into Chad and east toward the Nile.

On June 26, 1889, Michel Dolisie represented the French government at a ceremony on the Ubangi River. He met the local ruler of the river people. In a traditional ceremony, the two exchanged drops of blood and became blood brothers. Then they buried a lance and a rifle to symbolize their friendship and peaceful

cooperation. The site of the ceremony, Bangui, became the French capital of the river region.

In 1893 the first French missionaries arrived. They founded Mission Saint Paul of the Rapids. Soon tradesmen, both European and African, opened stores in the growing town of Bangui. French administrators followed the French troops. By 1909 Bangui was an apostolic prefecture (a missionary territory under a Roman Catholic priest). By 1910 Bangui had a European population of one hundred, and it was a thriving, though small, city.

CONSOLIDATION OF POWER

Both France and Belgium wanted to control the Ubangi River traffic, because this river gave access to the Nile and thus eventually to the Mediterranean Sea. In July 1894, the French formally declared the formation of Upper Oubangui. The next month the Belgians agreed to fix the border between French and Belgian territories along the M'Bomou River, ignoring the fact that this border cut right through existing Zande kingdoms.

In 1894 the French also established a military post at Berberati, and they pushed toward Chad. The French plan was to link their Congo River colony to their empire in West Africa and to the Nile River. Chad and the Central African Republic, which the French called Oubangui-Chari, were the final pieces to be fitted into the picture.

In July 1898, French forces (led by General J. B. Marchland) met the British (led by General Herbert Kitchener) at Fashoda on the Nile River. Both nations wanted to control the mighty Nile, with its outlet to the Mediterranean. The British claimed Fashoda as part of Egypt. They threatened war if the French did not retreat. For a while, it looked as if all Europe would be drawn into the Anglo-French conflict over African territories. But the French decided to withdraw. On March 21, 1899, they agreed to the boundary between the Sudan and Oubangui-Chari.

Although they had lost the Nile, the French had gained new colonial territory in Central Africa. Though they immediately proclaimed control, the French consolidated their power slowly. Not until 1912 was French influence felt at the village level.

Rabah Zubayr's troops fought the French in the north until Rabah's death in 1900. Three years later, a general revolt broke out in Mandjia areas in the west. The people were protesting the recruitment of porters to carry supplies to Chad. Whole regions had become depopulated because of the recruitment practices.

Revolts continued to plague the west from 1907 to 1909, when the French conquered it. In 1912 they also conquered the east, but only after defeating Senoussi, one of Rabah's followers. It had proved harder to overcome African resistance than to settle quarrels in Europe over colonial boundaries.

FRENCH EQUATORIAL AFRICA

In 1906 Oubangui-Chari and Chad were united to form one colony. Four years later, the French created French Equatorial Africa, which included Congo, Gabon, Chad, and Oubangui-Chari. A governor general in Brazzaville ruled French Equatorial Africa, and lieutenant governors represented him in each territo-

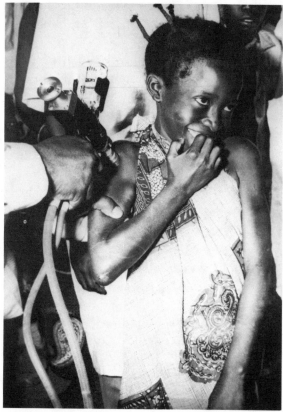

Many people died from contagious diseases and bad living conditions before modern medicine came to the Central African Republic.

ry. Appointed councils assisted the governor general and the lieutenant governors. Chad became a separate military territory in 1916 and a colony four years later.

The French changed the boundaries of Oubangui-Chari several times in the 1930s. The areas of Haute-Sangha and Lobaye were detached from French Congo and annexed to Oubangui-Chari. The Sara regions of Oubangui-Chari were placed under the jurisdiction of Chad. The Birao district remained part of Oubangui-Chari, because it gave the colony access to the Darfur region of the Sudan.

The French divided Oubangui-Chari-Chad into four basic units. The western region included land and people west of a line from Bangui to the Logone River. The eastern region included land and people east of a line from Bangui to the Darfur. The third region included the land and people between the other two. The fourth district was Bangui, the permanent capital after 1906.

Missionaries continued to expand their field of action. They attracted children into their missions and purchased and freed any slaves they found for sale. The Africans who lived at the mission or in "villages of liberty" studied and worked with the missionaries. They learned to read and write, to work with wood, and to grow food crops. The villages of liberty had individual family dwellings and fields of manioc, millet, maize, and bananas.

LIFE UNDER FRENCH RULE

The economic success of the Belgian companies in the Belgian Congo (present-day Zaïre) influenced the French government to offer special arrangements, called *concessions,* to French companies. Thirty-nine companies willing to invest in Oubangui-Chari received legal rights for thirty years over all natural resources except minerals in a given area. They had to pay the French government a fixed annual fee plus 15 percent of profits.

After the concession system was abandoned, the French government began to make food and agriculture one of its major concerns in Oubangui-Chari.

The concession system was a disaster for the colony. The companies lost money. Agents were frequently unskilled managers who mistreated the African workers. Africans were forced to grow cotton or coffee, collect rubber, or mine diamonds. They had no time and little energy to devote to their food crops.

Diseases ran through the laborers' camps and porters' villages. People not

Pierre de Brazza.

working for agricultural or mining companies were forcefully recruited as porters or road builders. Porters had to march at least fifteen miles, carrying sixty-six pounds of goods. For this they received one franc, but no food.

Forced-labor policies were possible in the early years of colonial development only because Africans still had food reserves. Later they had to live in supervised villages connected to a mine or a plantation and were allowed to visit their home villages only once a month. Crops died from neglect and wild animals feasted on unguarded fields. Those who remained in the villages were too ill, old, or young

to work in the mines or the plantations. But they were also too ill, old, or young to work the fields. Left alone in their home villages, they died of hunger or disease, particularly sleeping sickness or smallpox. Entire villages disappeared from the map of Central Africa.

Tales of some of these excesses reached Europe, and Pierre de Brazza was sent to Oubangui-Chari to investigate. His investigation confirmed the harsh rumors. But de Brazza died in Dakar on September 14, 1905, and his report was kept quiet. The ruthless exploitation of French Equatorial Africa came to be known as a system of "pillage economy."

By the 1920s, the population of Oubangui-Chari had dramatically declined, and the area's economy was worsening. The newly arrived governor of Oubangui-Chari, Auguste Lamblin, tried to correct the abuses of the concessions and strengthen the country. He rebuilt abandoned villages, set up plantations of food crops to stop the spread of famine, prohibited rubber gathering during harvest periods, and reduced the Africans' taxes. Lamblin declared the food supply to be one of the government's concerns. He also established an agricultural school for training Africans in the latest farming techniques. He regulated the porterage system, which had led to manhunts similar to the slave raids of earlier centuries.

Despite Lamblin's attempts at reform, harsh practices did not end. André Gide, a noted French author, wrote *Voyage to the Congo* in 1927 as a criticism of colonial conditions. Even then, workers were still forcibly recruited to build roads and railroads. The next year, the Baya people of the Haute-Sangha region rebelled against the labor requirements for the Congo-Ocean railroad from Brazzaville to Pointe Noire. The railroad was notorious because of the number of Africans who died of malnutrition, exposure, and overwork for each mile of track laid. The revolt lasted three years. Rebels managed to control Berberati, Bouar, Carnot, and Baibokoum (Chad) until the French forces overwhelmed them in 1931, a year after the railroad was completed.

No successful revolts occurred in the 1930s, when the French colonial system was in full force. It was not until the 1940s and World War II that French control was loosened. Now the Central Africans would have a chance to get out from under French control.

Central African Republic Today

WORLD WAR II OPENS THE WAY

For Oubangui-Chari, as for other colonial areas of the world, World War II marked the beginning of the modern era of national independence. French Equatorial Africa supported General Charles De-Gaulle and the Free French during the war, rather than the Nazi forces that occupied France. Oubangui-Chari sent soldiers to fight alongside the Allied armies in Libya, Ethiopia, Italy, France, and Germany. The Central African sharpshooter unit became particularly well known.

As Africans fought to free other peoples, they began to think seriously about restoring their own independent status. After the war, they claimed as their own the doctrine of self-determination, a doctrine reaffirmed at the postwar European peace conference. It stated that peoples should have the right to determine for themselves how they will be governed.

During World War II, Félix Eboué, a native of French Guiana (in South America) became governor general of French Equatorial Africa. He had spent twenty-five years in Oubangui-Chari. Eboué defended local customs and rights. In 1941 he formed a council of local interests in each territory. Many of Eboué's policies were reaffirmed at the 1944 Brazzaville Conference, an assembly of African delegates. The Brazzaville Conference also discussed the movement toward African self-determination.

Modern buildings in Bangui show how rapidly the Central African Republic has developed in the years since independence.

The French constitution of 1946 incorporated some ideas from the conference and created the French Union. Africans became French citizens and gained the right to decide local matters. But they did not have the choice of independence. The European colonists in French Africa did gain the right, however, to elect their own national assemblies and to send an elected deputy to the French National Assembly. Oubangui-Chari chose as its representative to the French Assembly Barthelemy Boganda who would lead the nation to the threshold of independence in 1960.

Deputies to the Oubangui-Chari assembly were elected by two electoral colleges. One included French colonists, who selected fourteen delegates. The other included African elite, who elected twenty-six delegates.

BARTHELEMY BOGANDA

Barthelemy Boganda was born into a farming family on April 4, 1910, in the Lobaye district. When his parents were killed by guards in charge of rubber gathering, Roman Catholic missionaries adopted Barthelemy, reared him, and educated him. On December 24, 1922, he was baptized a Christian. Barthelemy studied at St. Paul of the Rapids in Bangui. Then he took advanced studies in the Belgian Congo, in Brazzaville, and in Yaounde (Cameroon). On March 17, 1938, Boganda was ordained a Catholic priest, the first Oubanguian to be so ordained.

Boganda held several posts in Catholic missions. Meanwhile, his interest in politics was growing. After World War II, Boganda openly attacked the practices of the colonial administration and urged his fellow Africans to throw off the yoke of colonialism. Eventually, Boganda gave up the priesthood for the life of a politician.

When the opportunity came to send a representative to Paris to the French National Assembly, the people of Oubangui-Chari chose Boganda. He used his position as a deputy to speak out against the evils of colonialism. He urged the French Assembly to give equal rights to all men, including those in overseas territories. Boganda wanted France to achieve the unity of Christian and republican ideals. In the eyes of many Frenchmen, Boganda was simply an agitator and a nuisance. To his countrymen, he became a hero.

In 1948 Boganda founded the Cooperative Society of Lobaye-Lesse, the first in a series of producer and consumer cooperatives. His idea was to create an economic organization not dependent on French subsidies. The organization would also unite the people in a self-help effort. Unfortunately, Boganda knew little about economics, and his colleagues misused the cooperatives' funds. In 1951 the scheme had to be abandoned.

On January 10, 1951, the Lobaye cooperative had a dispute with some European traders over a business transaction. The Africans insisted on closing the market until Boganda arrived. Fearing a riot, the head of the district imprisoned Boganda and kept him in jail for forty-eight hours. On March 29 Boganda was sentenced to two months in jail; his French wife was sentenced to two weeks. The colonial authorities hoped they had silenced their most effective critic. But on the contrary, Boganda became a hero and martyr to his countrymen.

More successful than the cooperative was Boganda's political organization, Movement for Social Emancipation of Black Africa (MESAN). The aim of MESAN was to develop and liberate black Africans politically. Each community was to form its own committee.

French colonial leaders opposed this new political movement. To undercut MESAN's appeal, the French increased the price paid for African-grown cotton and established a few schools around the country. But the popularity of MESAN increased until it became a major political force.

THE BERBERATI RIOT

On April 30, 1954, an African cook and his wife, who had both worked for a European known for his cruelty, died in Berberati. A mob of Africans demanded the arrest of the European. When no arrest was made, they began to attack any European they saw. The governor of Berberati asked Boganda to intervene. On May 1 Boganda addressed the crowd, urging them to return to their homes. They obeyed him, even though the Baya town was not a center of strong support for Boganda.

A week later, the government arrested the rioters and the European. The rioters were given severe prison sentences. The accused European was cleared of all charges and freed.

Despite its outcome, the Berberati riot did not lead to other violent protests. But Boganda's party replaced the French People's Party (the Gaullist party) in most districts. Gradually, the administration recognized the inevitable, and officials made peace with Boganda and MESAN.

LOI CADRE

Boganda was elected to the local assembly in January of 1956. Six months later, the French National Assembly enacted the *loi cadre,* or enabling act, which gave colonial assemblies more control over their own affairs. In place of the two-college system, it established a single electorate.

The government of Oubangui-Chari formed in 1957 had more authority than its predecessors. The governor controlled local affairs and was also president of the government council. The local assembly elected the council. The grand council and general high commissioner still oversaw the external affairs of the four territories of French Equatorial Africa. In June 1957, Boganda became president of the Grand Council.

MESAN carried the election of all seats

in the territorial assembly. The Oubangui-Chari council had six ministers. The Minister of Agriculture was David Dacko, who would become the second president of the Republic. The Minister of Finance was Abel Goumba, who would lead the opposition against Dacko. Other posts included Minister of Social Services, Minister of Labor, Minister of Public Works, and Minister of Economics and Administration.

1958 REFERENDUM

In September of 1958, the French government held a referendum in its colonies. The colonists were asked to choose between complete independence or membership in a French Community led by France. Boganda had long advocated independence for his country, but he saw the need for maintaining ties with France for a while longer. If the country were to develop, he felt, it would need economic assistance from France. He traveled through Oubangui-Chari, urging the people to vote for joining the Community. On September 28, the people voted 98 percent in favor of the French Community. The other territories of French Equatorial Africa also voted to join the Community.

The French Community was based on the principle of free determination. All members of the Community became French citizens, with the right to elect the president of France and the deputies to the National Assembly. Each member state had its own elected assembly. France appointed the president and retained control of defense, foreign policy, and economic trade.

The government of Oubangui-Chari was reshuffled to prepare for its new responsibilities. Boganda became president, Abel Goumba became vice-president, and David Dacko became Minister of the Interior and the Economy.

In 1959 the Oubangui-Chari Assembly adopted a constitution that was modeled on the French constitution. The constitution created district councils, rural and urban boroughs, and mutual-development societies.

TOWARD INDEPENDENCE AND TRAGEDY

After 1958 the countries of French Equatorial Africa moved steadily toward full sovereignty. Boganda favored one unified state to replace French Equatorial Africa. He proposed that the new state be called the Central African Republic and that it be governed by a central council. The presidency would rotate among Oubangui-Chari, Gabon, Congo, and Chad. As a long-range goal, Boganda hoped for a federation of Latin Africa, including Belgian and Portuguese areas. Boganda's plans were soon halted by Gabon, which opposed any sort of unified government among the French Equatorial African states.

The Central African Republic's ties with France remained very strong even after independence. Here a French technical adviser (center) discusses a problem with his Central African counterpart.

On March 29, 1959, tragedy struck. Boganda left Berberati airport bound for Bangui. Somewhere on the short flight, the plane crashed and everyone on the airplane died. Goumba assumed the duties of presidency until a new leader could be selected to replace the beloved Boganda.

On April 30 David Dacko, Boganda's nephew, became president. Dacko was born on March 24, 1932, in Lobaye, son of a nightwatchman. Dacko attended school in Congo, became a teacher, and headed a school in Bangui. He was active in a teachers' union and in MESAN. In 1957 he won election to the territorial assembly. Dacko held three ministerial posts in Boganda's administration—agriculture, administrative affairs, and interi-

47

Left and below: Independence made the diverse peoples of Oubangui-Chari into a single state called Central African Republic.

CENTRAL AFRICAN REPUBLIC PHOTOGRAPHIC LIBRARY

or, economy, and commerce. In 1959 he was officially declared president of the Oubangui-Chari government.

A NEW NATION

Under Dacko, Oubangui-Chari continued its plans for full independence. On July 12, 1960, Dacko signed the agreement of cooperation and transfer of sovereignty. Full independence was declared in a torchlight ceremony on the evening of August 13. The new state called itself the Central African Republic, honoring the name Boganda had selected.

Although the sixty years of colonial rule had been only a brief episode in the long history of Central Africa, they left the region much changed. No longer an area of small autonomous settlements, Central Africa was now a centralized state containing many diverse peoples and cultures.

1960 CONSTITUTION

The first constitution of the independent republic was approved in November of 1960. The constitution provided for an Assembly and president elected by the people. Lawmaking was the function of the Assembly, which also gave the president his power. The sixty delegates were elected to five-year terms.

The president also served a five-year term. He had the power to name ministers, who were then responsible to him, and he presided over the Council of Ministers. The president also executed the laws of the Assembly, appointed public employees, headed the army, led the security forces, accredited ambassadors, and negotiated treaties.

The new state chose as its motto "Unity-Dignity-Work." Its flag is four horizontal bands of blue, white, green, and yellow, with a red vertical band running through the center and the five-pointed star of MESAN in the upper-left corner. The nation's anthem is "The Rebirth" *("La Renaissance"),* written by Boganda. Its words express the sentiment of the new republic:

O Central Africa! O cradle of the
   Bantus!
Take back your right to respect, to life!
For a long time subjugated,
   for a long time held down by all,
But from this day shattering tyranny.
In work, order, dignity
You regain your rights, your unity,
And to pass to this new stage
The voice from our ancestors calls us.
Chorus: To work in order and dignity
       In the respect of the right, in
       unity
       Shattering misery and tyranny,
       Brandishing the banner of the
       Fatherland.

The administration of the country below the national level was divided into twelve prefectures, thirty-seven subprefectures, and two autonomous subprefectures. The subprefect was similar to a district chief. He was in close communication with the citizens, and he supervised government programs. The prefect coordinated the efforts of the subprefects. Another group of officials—the inspectors—toured the districts and reported to the president.

Several urban centers—such as Bangui, Berberati, and Bambari—had their own elected governments. Rural collectives formed by groups of villages were administered by a council. The leader of the council was in charge of local production and police matters.

REVIVAL OF MESAN

Dacko's administration lasted five years and was plagued by opposition. Goumba resigned from the government in protest over Dacko's claim to power. In June 1960, Goumba founded the Movement of Democratic Evolution of Central Africa (MEDAC) to replace MESAN, which had deteriorated since Barthelemy Boganda's death. In November MEDAC tried to demonstrate against Dacko and his recent decrees, which concentrated power in his own hands. The crowd was dispersed and leaders arrested. In 1962 Goumba was tried and sentenced to life imprisonment. All opposition parties were banned. The French supported Dacko's repressive measures because they were frightened by the example of political breakdown in the nearby Belgian Congo (Zaïre).

Dacko moved quickly to rebuild MESAN into the mass organization it had been in Boganda's time. He ordered prefectures to appoint three delegates from each constituency to a national congress. In July 1962, the congress met and passed many resolutions, which the Assembly ratified. On paper, MESAN was once again a mass party. Yet Dacko seemed too closely allied with French business and government and MESAN officials were unpopular in the rural areas.

In 1964 Dacko was reelected president for a seven-year term, and the constitution was rewritten. The new constitution was based on the idea that MESAN was the nation's fountain of life. The party was to absorb all local organizations, such as youth clubs and trade unions. Everyone was a member of the party, and everyone had to pay dues. The party and the government became one; the budget of MESAN became part of the national budget.

The revised constitution recognized three social levels. The president was at the top. A national elite would hold all posts of responsibility. The working class (the lowest social level) would continue to perform their daily jobs. Party leaders would settle any disputes at the local level. Presidents of MESAN districts were automatically presidents of local government councils.

UNWISE ECONOMIC DECISIONS

Dacko was conscious of the fact that

fifty Frenchmen still held positions of power in the Republic. Eager to "Africanize" the government, in 1961 he replaced the foreigners with Africans. At the same time, he increased the number of civil-service positions and raised their salaries. The Republic's economy was strained by this increase in administrative expenses. Taxes were increased to pay for the luxurious lifestyle of high government officials.

Dacko gave a joint stock company (the National Diamond Company) the monopoly to purchase diamonds. He exempted this company from duties, even though the duty revenue was critical to the government's treasury. In the early 1960s, diamond output rose. In 1965 Dacko gave out other licenses for mining diamonds without consulting the company. Finally, he suspended licensing authority completely. Villagers were permitted to mine and sell diamonds that were not in the territory of mining companies.

Villages and fields fell into disrepair as people searched for diamonds. A farmer could make much more money in a few weeks of diamond mining than in months of cotton cultivating. Confusion reigned in mining areas, and outbreaks of violence occurred. Cotton production fell to its lowest point in years. The cotton crop was disastrous in 1965, and Dacko imposed a forced-labor system similar to that of colonial days.

COUP D'ETAT

By 1965 the Central African Republic was ripe for a *coup d'état* (government overthrow). The countries near the Republic also were in turmoil. The former Belgian Congo (Zaïre) to the south was in a state of civil war. Rebellions broke out in the Sudan, sending a flood of refugees into the Central African Republic. Chad faced the threat of a violent change in government.

The final push for the ouster of Dacko came in December of 1965. Dacko proposed a budget that required all civil servants, but not high government officials, to take a 10 percent salary cut. This was supposed to help the nation's general economic condition. Dissatisfaction was evident everywhere in Bangui, and the chief of police planned to seize political power on New Year's Eve.

Colonel Jean-Bedel Bokassa learned of the plot. He invited the chief of police to his home, then arrested him. Next Bokassa initiated his own coup. He had already complained about reduced funding for the army. Now he sent soldiers to surround the presidential palace. Dacko was persuaded to resign the presidency in favor of Colonel Bokassa. Meanwhile, opponents of the Dacko regime were sacking the mansions of high-ranking ministers. Some of the ministers were taken to military camps and imprisoned.

On January 1, 1966, Bokassa announced to the country that a new regime was in force. He released Dacko's political prisoners. Bokassa also dissolved the National Assembly and ignored the constitu-

President Bokassa built this marketplace at Bangui and named it for himself.

tion. He set up a Revolutionary Council to handle administrative decision-making. The council was composed of three former ministers, three army officers, and three young civil servants. In their enthusiasm over the change in regimes, the people called Bokassa "the warrior who had given himself to the service of his abandoned people."

JEAN-BEDEL BOKASSA

Bokassa was born on February 22, 1921, in Lobaye. He was a relative of Boganda. When Bokassa was six years old, his father died from ill treatment at the hands of the French. Shortly thereafter, his mother committed suicide out of grief. Roman Catholic missionaries took care of

CENTRAL AFRICAN REPUBLIC

Birao

VAKAGA

BAMINGUI-
BANGORAN

N'dele

UPPER
KOTTO

OUHAM-
PENDE

OUHAM

KEMO-
GRIBINGUI

Bozoum · Bassangoa

Bouar ·

Bria ·

UPPER
MBOMOU

OUAKA

NANA-
MAMBERE

OMBELLA-
MPOKO

Fort
Sibut

Bambari ·

Yakotoko ·

MBOMOU

Boali ·

BANGUI ⊛

LOWER
KOTTO

Bangassou ·

Berberati ·

LOBAYE

Mobaye ·

UPPER
SANGHA

M'Baiki ·

PREFECTURES

Bokassa's picture and name are everywhere in the Central African Republic.

young Bokassa and educated him.

At eighteen, Bokassa joined the French army and was stationed in North Africa and then in Indochina. By 1956 he was a second lieutenant. When Dacko became president in 1960, he asked Bokassa to form a war cabinet. Bokassa became chief of staff and a major in 1963. Less than three years later, he was president of the Republic.

BOKASSA'S REGIME

Bokassa's declared policy was to improve the daily life of Central Africans. To this end he donated funds to hospitals, built covered markets, raised the school-leaving age for girls to twenty years of age, abolished legal polygamy (having more than one wife), ordered transport vehicles from France, and subsidized orchestras. The new president wanted to modernize farming and livestock production, increase diamond production, develop uranium mines, build railroads and roads, and expand the nation's export trade. Production of cotton, coffee, timber, and diamonds increased, but rising import costs enlarged the trade deficit. By 1970 the economic position was worsening.

Meanwhile, fearful of plots to overthrow him, in 1967 Bokassa asked the French to send troops into the Republic. This move was generally unpopular. The same year, Bokassa took over the Ministry of the Interior. He retained control of the Ministry of Defense. In August he became secretary general of MESAN.

In 1968 Bokassa promoted himself to the rank of brigadier general. The next year he accused his vice-president, Lieutenant Colonel Alexandre Banza, of plotting a coup d'état. Banza was executed, along with other officers. Bokassa reorganized the Council of Ministers.

The National Pioneer Youth, created in 1962, became a paramilitary organization seven years later. Its leader was Bokassa. At its peak, membership in forty clubs reached seven thousand.

The early 1970s were hard times for the Bokassa regime. The president arbitrarily ordered the mines closed, French economic experts were expelled from the country. Fraud brought agricultural cooperatives to the brink of collapse. Bokassa hoped that offers of aid would come from Eastern Europe, but he was disappointed. The Republic received little assistance.

In 1971 the Council of Ministers was reshuffled and enlarged to twenty-four members. Bokassa expanded and almost doubled the size of the army and promoted himself to full general. In March 1972 Bokassa was named "President for Life."

In April 1973 the government was reshuffled again. Auguste M'Bongo, second in power in the cabinet, was accused of plotting a coup d'état and imprisoned. Bokassa took charge of the Ministry of Agriculture, Trade, Industry, and Mines and the Ministry of Transportation.

Late in 1974 Bokassa announced the further strengthening of his authority. He became field marshal and assumed control of the Ministry of Civil Aviation and Aeronautics. Today President Bokassa rules by decree. His council consists of nine ministers of state, ten ministers, and three secretaries of state. But these officials exist only to express the will of Marshal and "President for Life" Bokassa. The country was reorganized into fourteen prefectures. Officials are appointed by the Council and report to the Minister of the Interior—Bokassa.

In 1977 Bokassa proclaimed himself Emperor and renamed his country the Central African Empire. He has ordered a jeweled crown made for himself.

INTERNATIONAL RELATIONS

As independence approached in 1960, the members of French Equatorial Africa agreed to maintain their ties of association. The prime ministers of Chad, Congo, and the Central African Republic agreed to form the Union of Central African Republics. The Union had jurisdiction over foreign relations, defense, communications, and currency. Gabon, also a former French colony, would not join the Union.

The prime ministers of the Union and Gabon agreed to meet at regular intervals. They called their meetings the Conference of Heads of State. The Conference agreed to maintain communications, to set up a permanent secretariat, and to establish a customs union. The four nations agreed to act as a body in negotiations with the European Economic Community and the General Agreement on Tariffs and Trade.

In February of 1964 the governments of the Union of Central African Republics, plus Gabon this time, agreed to strengthen their bonds. They would cooperate on road construction and the establishment of an oil refinery in Port-Gentil (Gabon). On December 8, 1964, the five countries created a new Customs Union of Central African States (UDEAC). The members agreed in December 1967 to coordinate their tax laws, create a commission to study higher education, and ask the World Bank to establish field offices inside the Union. The Republic had joined the World Bank and the International Monetary Fund in 1963.

In the early 1960s the Republic had joined eleven other African governments to form the African and Malagasy Union (UAM). In February 1965, UAM was re-formed. The Republic and twelve other French-speaking states agreed to form the Common African and Malagasy Union (OCAM). Its charter was approved in June of 1966.

In 1971 OCAM became the Afro-Malagasy-Mauritian Common Organization. Today its ten members share a postal system, telecommunications, a merchant fleet, Air Afrique airlines, and customs and tariff regulations. On August 12, 1974, OCAM members decided to make Bangui its headquarters.

In 1968 the Central African Republic, Zaïre, and Chad attempted a new political union, the Union of Central African States (UEAC). They merged their airlines and agreed to exchange defense information and coordinate defense efforts. Gabon and the People's Republic of the Congo were asked but refused to join. The Central African Republic withdrew from UDEAC to join UEAC. The new political union was shortlived, though. On December 9, 1968, Bokassa withdrew his nation from UEAC and rejoined UDEAC. Thereafter, the Central African Republic had minor disputes with both Chad and Zaïre.

Almost as soon as it became independent, the Republic established ties with the United States, the Soviet Union, West Germany, Israel, and Taiwan. In 1962 the Republic signed an agreement of economic cooperation with Israel. The next year, it negotiated with Taiwan for a team of rice experts to come to Bangui. In 1964 the Republic signed a general cooperative agreement with Taiwan and

The former palace of the president of the Central African Republic nestles on the hills outside Bangui.

began to solicit aid from the Eastern Bloc.

In the late 1960s, the Soviet Union signed a scientific cooperation agreement, a trade agreement, and a general cultural agreement. The Republic and the Soviet Union also negotiated an agreement to exchange delegations in medicine, teaching, sports, and arts.

David Dacko recognized the People's Republic of China in 1964 and obtained, on paper, a loan of one billion CFA francs. (The CFA franc is the common currency of the Union of Central African Republics.) But when Bokassa took over in 1966, he expelled the Chinese. The one billion CFA francs were never received.

Israel maintained an embassy in Bangui until October 21, 1973, when the Republic broke diplomatic ties with Israel as a result of Arab-Israeli warfare. The Republic, like many other African states, decided to side with the Arabs.

The Central African Republic joined the United Nations on September 20, 1960. Today in Bangui there are twenty-five accredited diplomatic missions and eight non-resident accredited missions.

EDUCATION

During the colonial era, only 5 percent of school-age children attended school. Today more than 50 percent are students in primary schools. About 75 percent of school-age boys have been to school; for girls the figure is 25 percent. The schools are run by the government and are taught very much like French schools. French is also the language of instruction.

There are about 170,000 pupils attending 780 primary schools that have 2,600 teachers. About 10,000 students attend the 20 secondary schools. There are almost 400 secondary-school teachers. About 1,500 students are in technical schools, and another 550 are studying abroad at universities.

The government wants to increase the number of primary schools, especially in small villages. It also concentrates on developing the teacher-training school and technical-training institutions. In Bangui there is a National School of Administration, a School of Arts and Crafts, and a nursing school. An agricultural school is located elsewhere.

In February 1970, the University of Jean-Bedel Bokassa began operation in Bangui. It has a faculty (school) of law and economy, a faculty of letters and humanities, a faculty of medicine, and a faculty of science.

LITERATURE

Central Africa is more noted for its traditional oral histories, folktales and other stories, and proverbs than for written literature. This is partly because the local languages did not have written alphabets. Perhaps the best known work by an author from the Republic is Pierre Bambote's *Funeral Chant for a Hero of Africa,* published in 1962.

Some often-quoted Central African proverbs sound very much like sayings from anywhere in the world: "Better nine as a gift than ten as a promise"; "When the cat is absent, the rats are master"; "The curse of the hen does not touch the hawk"; "War among grasshoppers delights the cows."

Opposite top: Children play outside their modern school building. Opposite bottom: At this school the children practice their writing on small chalkboards.

Natural Treasures

ABUNDANT WILDLIFE

A large, dark-brown head rises above the waters of the Ubangi River. It has small eyes, no visible ears, and a thick upper lip covered with bristles. A fusiform body (tapering toward each end) about ten feet long and covered with short bristles soon appears. After a few moments on the surface for a breath of air, the creature dives underwater and begins to nibble the aquatic plants along the river bottom. Two front flippers and a flat tail move the creature through the water at a leisurely pace. This is the manatee, or sea cow, a harmless mammal that inhabits the Ubangi River.

Other inhabitants of the river regions are less exotic. Along the shores live crocodiles, hippopotamuses, and numerous waterfowl. Many types of fish swim in the stream.

Because of the varied terrain and climate, the Central African Republic has an abundance of animal, bird, and insect life. The most numerous animals are the primates—monkeys and apes. They share the savanna region with buffalo, elephants, lions, cheetahs, hyenas, and antelopes. Only a few giraffes, rhinoceroses, and ostriches live within the borders of the country.

The tropical forests have a wildlife all their own. Giant squirrels, brightly colored birds, butterflies, snakes, and bats are numerous. The bird population also in-

This stuffed gorilla at a Central African museum "holds hands" with one of the museum's technicians. It is an excellent example of taxidermy.

cludes pigeons, eagles, owls, and sparrows. Reptiles of the forest include chameleons, lizards, vipers, and pythons.

Termites, ants, grasshoppers, and tsetse flies are common insects in the Republic. The tsetse fly, slightly larger than a housefly, is the most dangerous to human beings and domestic animals. It transmits the disease called sleeping sickness, or trypanosomiasis. The fly lives in wooded areas and has a lifespan of one to three months. It feeds by biting humans or animals and sucking their blood. The fly feeds almost daily and especially likes to eat during the brightest, warmest, hours. Because of its prevalence it is difficult to raise livestock in most of tropical Africa.

PLANT LIFE

Tropical forests cover about 10 percent of the Central African Republic. At least two hundred kinds of hardwoods grow in the southern rain forest. Various types of mahogany and ebony are the best-known of these woods, though limba and acajou are also abundant.

One of the Central African Republic's most beautiful natural treasures is this rushing waterfall.

The limba tree grows to a great height. The lower part of the trunk is completely free of branches. The crown of the tree is a broad, flat carpet of green, composed of upright clusters of leaves on horizontal branches. The wood is pale yellow near the bark, but the heartwood is veined in black or wholly brown-black. This tree is used in the manufacture of veneers.

Other useful trees that grow in abundance in the forest are cacao, kola nut, and pepperplants. Beautiful flowers also grow everywhere in the rain forest. Perhaps the best-known flower is the porcelain rose.

The savanna region produces karité, acacia, gum arabic, and coffee trees. The karité tree is particularly important for its fruit, which has an oily kernel—a major source of fat in the local diet.

Wild dates, figs, and locust trees grow in the northern area. The locust tree, also called the carob tree, grows to a height of fifty feet. It has glossy, evergreen leaves and yellow or red flowers. Flat, leathery pods contain hard, brown seeds. The pods sometimes reach a length of twelve inches. The pods are about 50 percent sugar and are used for animal feed or human food.

MINERAL WEALTH

Three important minerals—diamonds, gold, and uranium—are known to exist in the Central African Republic. The first two have been mined for many years. Gold was discovered near Bambari in 1912. The next year diamonds were found near Ippy. Diamonds have since been mined in the Ouaka and Haute-Sangha regions. One of the largest diamonds found in the Republic weighed almost four hundred carats.

Uranium deposits are known to exist, but because the ore contains impurities, mining has been delayed. The reserves in the west are estimated to have about ten thousand tons of metal. There are also some uranium deposits near Bakouma.

Other known mineral resources include graphite, titanium, galena, iron, nickel, manganese, cobalt, tin, copper, and mercury. Stone, gravel, and clay are also useful resources for building construction.

Geologists are still exploring the varied regions of the Republic. They may yet discover mineral riches which today remain unknown to Central Africans.

The People Live in Central African Republic

ANCIENT RESIDENTS

There are more than fifty ethnic groups in the Central African Republic. Most of these groups are relative newcomers, but two groups—the pygmies and the river people—were among the original inhabitants of the region.

The pygmies moved their settlements deep into the forest to escape the waves of Bantu-speaking peoples. Although they adapted well to forest life, today only a few thousand pygmies remain. Like their ancestors, they are hunters and gatherers. They trade with nearby farmers to obtain foods and household goods.

The river peoples include several ethnic groups that live along the Ubangi River and in nearby forests. During the era of slave raids and great migrations, the river peoples retreated to islands for safety, but they maintained their control of the river trade. The Boubangui, Sango, M'Baka, Banziri, and other river peoples form only a small percentage of the country's total population, but they have made important contributions to life in the Republic. About 60 percent of all civil servants are from these groups. All three presidents have been M'Baka. Sango is one of the two official national languages (French is the other). Today many river people make their living as fishermen, traders, craftsmen, or government officials. They still maintain ties with their families and with other members of their age group.

A modern Central African family shows the contrast between Western influences and African traditions.

This man wears the traditional masks and headdress of his ethnic group.

NINETEENTH-CENTURY ARRIVALS

Many waves of people entered the Republic to escape slave raiders to the north and east. Two of the largest ethnic groups to do this were the Baya-Mandjia and the Banda. The Baya-Mandjia settled in the west and central sections of the country. The Banda moved into the eastern and central areas. The Sara and Bororo people stayed in the northern areas, close to their relatives in what is now Chad. Original inhabitants of the Republic either married into these groups, moved south, or died in warfare.

Neither the Baya nor the Banda developed organized states. During the dangerous times, when they were being threatened from the outside and needed strong leadership to organize their defense, the Baya and Banda selected war leaders. But the authority of the leaders lasted only until peace returned. In times of peace, the leaders served only as mediators or judges. They had no official position during peacetime.

THE BAYA-MANDJIA

Even today, as before, the Baya-Mandjia are not highly organized politically. Consensus (similar to majority opinion) rules. Everyone is encouraged to express his opinion at local village meetings.

The society is organized around clans and nuclear families. Each clan includes families with a particular ancestor in common. The clans are ruled by elders, who hold the real power in the society. The elder controls farmland, organizes hunting and fishing expeditions, arranges marriages, and settles succession disputes. He is also a priest charged with fertility of the soil.

Land and trade goods belong to the clan, not to individuals. Each individual in the clan has a specific place in society. Even the dead are still considered part of the clan.

The nuclear family is the basis of the social structure. Since the society is patriarchal, descent is counted only through the male line. In fact, children of a daughter are not considered relatives by their maternal grandparents!

The male family head owns everything in the household except his wife's jewelry. When a son leaves home, he may take some implements he used in his work for his father. When a daughter leaves, she takes some kitchen equipment.

THE BANDA

Before modern times, the Banda were noted for their facial scars, elaborate tattoos, and lip ornaments. Banda men inserted a wooden or ivory disk in their upper lip and filed their teeth. The women wore elaborate jewelry—pearl necklaces, bracelets of copper or ivory, spirals on the arms and legs, and metal nose rings.

Today the Banda are less likely to decorate their bodies in the traditional manner, though they have kept much of their heritage. They are organized into family groups rather than a centralized government. They are still a society of hunters, fishermen, and farmers.

This field, like so much of the Republic's farmland, is probably owned by an entire village rather than by one individual farmer.

These city babies, posing for the camera outside a day-care center, might never experience their people's traditional ways of life.

Land is the possession of the entire group and not an individual's property. Whoever farms a field, however, becomes its proprietor until he leaves the land. Then the fields revert to general ownership. Individuals do own their own houses, crops, working tools, weapons, personal items, and livestock.

There is some specialization of tasks among the Banda. Blacksmiths make jewelry, weapons, and tools. Artisans create drums, boats, and jewelry. Weavers prepare cloth and baskets. Fishermen produce their own nets and lines. Other craftsmen specialize in musical instruments.

The skills of farming and house building are universal. The main crops of the Banda are manioc, corn, and millet, but they also cultivate sweet potatoes, beans, and peanuts. One of their main meals is made from manioc. First, the manioc is mashed into a paste. The paste is mixed with vegetables, meat, fish, or termites, and seasoned with palm oil. The mixture is cooked in boiling water. A similar dish is made from millet flour.

Banda houses are round structures of wood, grasses, and adobe. The diameter of the house is usually fifteen to twenty feet. The interior has two rooms, one for cooking and eating and one for sleeping. The doorway is usually three feet wide. Some houses have pointed roofs, while the roofs of others are rounded.

A man preparing to build a new house

first traces an outline of the floor plan on the ground. Then he drives stakes into the ground around the circular outline. He cuts forks in the tops of poles, lays crossbeams in the notched places, and secures the beams with vines. The builder weaves small branches and twigs in and out around the poles. Then he plasters the walls inside and outside with adobe. Branches and reeds make the roof, which is sloped and thick enough to shed rain.

The Banda decorate their homes with elaborate designs. First, they paint the outside of the house white. Then they paint scenes that depict hunting expeditions, village life, mining scenes, or animal behavior. They make their paints from vegetable juices.

BANDA CEREMONIES

Religious ceremonies are very important to the Banda. There are ceremonies for birth, death, marriage, illness, and warfare. The Banda also perform ritual acts related to their daily chores of hunting, fishing, or farming.

The Banda live close to nature. They believe that spirits are present in the natural world. Some of the spirits are good and some are evil. To protect themselves against evil spirits, the Banda wear amulets around their waists, wrists, or ankles.

A rural woman walks from her village to her garden. In much of Africa the women of a village are responsible for growing certain crops and the men are responsible for others.

MICHAEL ROBERTS

Families have fetishes (containers of magic and powerful medicine) to protect the household. Clans have animal benefactors, called *totems*. The Banda believe that in past centuries their ancestors made a pact with the totem animal. Since that day, no clan member may kill the animal or eat its flesh.

The Banda believe that a benevolent genie takes charge of an individual at the moment of his conception. The same genie follows him through life. At the moment of death, the spirits take over. The spirits of the dead are believed to appear only at night. They return to the world of the living for food offerings, which show that the living still think well of their an-

Both American jazz and traditional African rhythms are popular forms of music in the Republic.

cestors. If the living neglect their duties toward the ancestors, the spirits deal severely with them. The Banda say that one can feel the presence of the spirits in dreams, in illness, in the actions of animals, and even in the wind.

Because of the importance of dead ancestors, ceremonies connected with burials are elaborate. The dead person is wrapped in white cloth and placed on a raised platform. The relatives of the deceased, also wearing white, dance all night to honor the dead. Then they sleep in the crouched position that the body will have in the grave.

Ceremonies surrounding birth are equally elaborate. A newborn child is anointed with oil and rubbed with powdered redwood. The child receives one name at birth. Other names are given the child at the time of circumcision and initiation into adulthood. Until a child is old enough to walk, he or she is carried in a skin-sling over the mother's left hip. Amulets protect the young child from evil spirits.

Banda children are initiated into adulthood between the ages of ten and fourteen. Preparation studies used to take several years, but now the time is considerably shorter. The children live together outside the village for months while studying Banda traditions and values. They wear ceremonial clothes and ornaments during this time. They listen to their elders tell stories of the ancestors and the clan history, and they learn the ways of the animals. They study the moral values of society. An initiate learns, for example, that a Banda should not lie or steal, but should act courageously in times of danger; and in times of hunger, a Banda should feed those whose crops have failed.

Initiated young women continue to live with their mothers until they marry. Young male initiates are given their own houses immediately after the ceremony. In order to marry, a young man must give his fiancée's family many items of value, such as tools, weapons, jewelry, or cash. It is seen as compensation to the bride's family for the loss of a valued person.

THE AZANDE

The Azande are a mixture of many ethnic groups that began to intermarry in the eighteenth century. Their main pursuits are farming and hunting. Azande craftsmen make sculpture out of wood, clay, and iron.

The staple crop of the Azande is eleusine grass, but they also grow maize, peanuts, sweet potatoes, sesame, peas, beans, manioc, and bananas. An important ingredient in their diet is oil crushed from termites.

The Azande live in scattered homesteads, and polygamy (having more than one wife) is common. In the past, a groom had to exchange twenty spears for his bride. Members of royal clans tend to marry within their own clan, while members of commoner clans may marry outside their own clan.

Children learn good dental habits as the Central African Republic works to improve the health of its people. The words above the chalkboard are the motto of the Republic: "Unity—dignity—work."

MEDICINE AND SOCIAL WELFARE

Central Africans can make use of many services provided by youth organizations, government agencies, and the military. Yet one major problem area remains—health care.

Diseases such as leprosy, bilharzia, malaria, trypanosomiasis (sleeping sickness) and hookworm threaten the people's well being. The Central African Republic has only thirty-six doctors, and all but two of these are foreigners. To support them are six hundred nurses, fifty technical nurses, and two hundred assistant nurses.

There are thirty-six district hospitals and maternity centers, one hundred dispensaries, and two hundred first-aid stations. The hospitals have a total of twenty-three hundred beds; nearly one-fourth of these are in Bangui. Mobile health units travel to all parts of the country during epidemics, but there are not enough personnel to treat everyone quickly.

The government has plans to upgrade its health services. It wants to expand the number of hospital beds, purchase modern operating equipment, and encourage more Central Africans to study medicine.

MUSLIMS

Only a small percentage of Central Africans are Muslims. Most of these people live in the north. The Muslims are native Africans who intermarried with the Arabs that controlled the region in past centuries. They were converted to the Arabs' religion, called Islam.

Many Sara and Bororo people are Muslims. They earn their living by raising cattle and a few crops. Ninety percent of all the cattlekeepers in the Republic are Bororo.

There is also a Muslim quarter in the capital city, Bangui. It is the most traditional, least-Westernized section of the city. Unlike the residents of other sections of the city, the Muslims tend to reject European lifestyles and cling to their traditional customs. They practice traditional crafts, such as leatherworking and embroidery, and craftspeople are organized into groups similar to guilds. Apprentices live with the master craftsman and learn his trade by observation and practice.

The People Work in Central African Republic

AGRICULTURE AND INDUSTRY

Farming has always been essential to the life of Central Africans. In precolonial days, village life followed the farming cycle of preparing the fields, planting, weeding, and harvesting.

During the colonial era, the French required the people to cultivate export crops, especially rubber, cotton, and coffee. Tobacco was introduced in 1925. The French granted certain rights, called *concessions,* to companies willing to develop agricultural production or oversee the gathering of palm kernels, sesame seeds, ivory, wax, and copal gum for export.

Today farming in the Republic is largely subsistence farming (growing crops for one's own use). About 85 percent of Central Africans are farmers. Their main staple is manioc, a starchy root that grows to a length of three feet. Its diameter varies from six to nine inches. Sweet manioc contains no hydrocyanic acid and may be eaten without danger, but bitter manioc must be treated.

Popular food grains are millet, sorghum, and corn. Peanuts, bananas, sweet potatoes, rice, and coffee are also important crops. Popular fruits and vegetables include green beans, peppers, cucumbers, pineapples, papayas, mangoes, guavas, and tangerines.

Different ethnic groups prefer to grow different crops. The Banda like to raise

These logs, identified and numbered, lie on the riverbank at Bangui. They will be transported to Kinshasa, Zaïre, and from there to major ports throughout the world.

millet, which has a six-month growing season. The river people cultivate millet, too, but they also like manioc, corn, and rice. The Baya-Mandjias prefer manioc, which takes eighteen months to mature. The Sara of the north grow millet, peanuts, and corn.

Cotton and coffee are the two main export crops. Cotton exports are the major source of foreign exchange, which the Republic needs to pay for imported goods. Cotton production doubled between 1965 and 1970 under a successful plan called "Operation Bokassa," and it peaked at 58,700 tons a year. After 1970, however, production declined by 10 percent a year because of bad weather and the removal of French technical advisers.

The Cotton Union of Central Africa now handles the purchase, transportation, and sale of the cotton. It has also reorganized the cotton gins and oil mills and has instituted more modern processing methods.

Most of the Republic's cotton farms are in Ouham, Ouham-Pendé, Ouaka, and Kemo-Gribingui prefectures. The cities of Bouar and Bambari are cotton centers. Cotton farmers meet at the cotton buyer's office to sell their harvest. The fee to be paid is set by the government. The buyer weighs the cotton for each farmer, figures the total price, and pays the individual farmer. While awaiting their turns at the weighing station, the farmers exchange news, purchase needed items, or take part in sports or amusements.

A government tax officer is usually present at the buyer's office to collect the government's share of the cotton fee. A judge is also there to settle any disputes that may arise. Merchants display their best wares in the hope of enticing the farmers to spend part of their new wealth before returning to their homes.

Coffee is the second-most important export crop. Excelsa coffee was native to the Central African Republic, but a disease killed the plants in 1937. In the late 1940s, the French introduced robusta and java coffee in Lobaye and Upper Sangha prefectures. In 1950 a disease-resistant excelsa plant was developed and planted in the Republic.

The Republic has many other industries that are vital to the daily lives of its population. These industries process raw materials into consumer goods. Of these, the textile industry ranks first in importance. There are twenty-one cotton gins and two textile factories in the Republic. At the textile factories in Bangui and Boali, thread is spun and woven and cloth is printed and dyed.

Other industries process foods. There are five vegetable-oil mills that press peanuts and palm fruit to extract the oil. The oil is used for cooking purposes. Two plants roast coffee beans. The slaughterhouse in Bangui handles fifteen thousand head of cattle a year, and a new slaughterhouse under construction will more than double the capacity of the meat-producing industry.

At other factories cattle feed is made, grain is ground into flour, and soap, paint, bricks, plastic bottles, and plastic sandals are all manufactured. At still other plants leather is tanned and approximately 750,000 pairs of shoes are produced each year. About a dozen sawmills cut 15,000,000 board feet of lumber a year for local construction and for export.

Consumer goods made in other countries are put together at assembly plants in the Central African Republic. Bicycles, motorcycles, radios, and kitchen equipment are some of these goods. Other shops import spare parts to repair machinery sold in the Republic.

Bangui and Boali are the Republic's main industrial centers. Bangui has at least fourteen kinds of industries. In the city are a cotton-cloth factory, a refrigerated slaughterhouse, an oil mill, a soap factory, a flour mill, a shoe factory, an animal-feed plant, a transistor-radio assembly plant, a bicycle assembly plant, a brewery, a food-processing plant, and an ice-making plant. There are many construction companies and transport companies as well.

Boali has fewer industries than Bangui but it can still boast of an electric power plant and a large textile complex, complete with weaving, cleaning, and dyeing operations. It also has coffee mills, soap factories, and oil-processing plants.

FISHING AND LIVESTOCK-RAISING

Some of the river people have become professional fishermen. They use sophisti-

CENTRAL AFRICAN REPUBLIC PHOTOGRAPHIC LIBRARY

Because so much cotton is grown there, the Central African Republic has a rapidly growing textile industry. Here, freshly made cotton fabric is coming off the machine.

cated equipment to catch fish, particularly the captaine, found in the Ubangi River. In special ponds they breed tilapia, an excellent-tasting fish and good source of protein.

Successful livestock-raising is impossible in the south, where the tsetse fly thrives, for sleeping sickness kills the cattle. In the northern regions, however, the Sara and the Bororo raise several types of animals. These peoples own about 350,000 head of cattle and 80,000 sheep. It is estimated that in the entire country there are 500,000 head of zebu cattle, more than 500,000 goats, about 56,000 pigs, and more than 1,000,000 chickens. But the meat from these animals that is processed in local slaughterhouses is not enough to meet local demands. Thus, many animals are imported every year from Chad.

MINING

Mining is one of the oldest industries in the Central African Republic. Diamonds and gold have been mined for generations, but known gold reserves are almost exhausted. In fact, gold mining ceased to be profitable in the 1950s. More than 60 percent of the diamonds mined in the Republic are of jewelry quality. There is a diamond-cutting factory in Bangui. Diamond production peaked at 609,000 carats in 1968. Production declined after 1970, when the large mining companies began to close.

Other minerals that may soon be mined include graphite, manganese, titanium, tin, galena, uranium, and iron. Iron reserves total seven hundred thousand tons. Uranium reserves were estimated to contain ten thousand tons of ore. But in the early 1970s, the ore was found to contain a high phosphate content. More recent estimates expect a yield of five thousand tons.

COMMERCE AND TRADE

Long-distance trade has long been a part of life in Central Africa. In centuries gone by, caravans from the Mediterranean coast and the Red Sea crossed Central Africa, passed through the Bangui region, and traded along the Ubangi-Zaïre rivers. The merchants brought salt, metals, pearls, and cloth to trade, returning home with ivory, gold, and diamonds. Traditional trade routes followed the Sangha, Lobaye, and Ubangi rivers. Another route linked Kouango to trade routes in present-day Ouaka and Upper Kotto prefectures. Caves along these routes still contain the remains of early campsites.

Today commerce in the Republic is centered on Bangui, yet it still crosses Central Africa and follows the rivers. Import-export companies have their headquarters in Bangui. Larger towns throughout the Republic have wholesale centers. Villages have their local marketplaces and retail stores. Main trade routes link Bangui to Pointe Noire (Congo) and Berberati to Brazzaville (Congo).

The Central African Republic must import many of its necessities, such as oil and lubricants, construction materials, appliances, machinery, and spare parts. It also imports some foods, beverages, dairy products, and sugar. Its main supplier is France, which sends Central Africans more than half of the imports they receive. Other suppliers are the United States, West Germany, Israel, England, the Netherlands, and Japan.

Since the Central African Republic lacks a seaport, imported goods must travel hundreds of miles from the ocean to reach distribution points. Transportation charges add much to the retail costs paid by Central Africans. Some items triple in price between the coast and Bangui. Government officials hope that when railroads linking Bangui to coastal cities in Congo and Cameroon are built, the problem of high costs will be lessened.

The Republic exports raw products to many countries, including the United States, Israel, and some European nations. France buys more than 50 percent of the Republic's exports. Diamonds, cotton, and coffee account for 90 percent of the value of Central African exports. Other products sent abroad include peanuts, palm products, rubber, ivory, tobacco, and sisal. The Republic's balance of payments is frequently negative. In 1971, for example, the nation's exports had a value of 8,939,000,000 CFA francs—or more than 100,000,000 francs less than the value of its imports.

TRANSPORTATION

Within the Republic, almost four hundred miles of navigable waterways are open all year. However, many of the tributary streams are overgrown and choked with weeds. Boat travel is difficult along the Kotto and Ouaka rivers for this reason. Sections of streams that are navigable in the rainy season often turn to dry beds the rest of the year.

During the late 1940s, river transport was improved along the Ubangi River near Bangui. Parts of the river were dredged, and some boulders were removed. Two transport companies handled river traffic.

In 1959 river traffic came under the joint supervision of the four republics of what had been French Equatorial Africa. Today the Central African Republic controls its own river transport system, though it cooperates with its neighbors.

The port facilities of Bangui include the old port with its three breakwaters and a new port downstream with one breakwater. At Kolongo, three miles from Bangui, is an oil port equipped with six pipelines.

Although the Republic presently has no railroad, plans are underway to build one to Douala (on the Cameroon coast) to handle freight shipments. It is hoped that modern rural towns will develop along this route at intervals of thirty or so miles. The Sudan and Central African Republic have agreed to build a railroad from Darfur, in the Sudan, to Vaga prefecture in the northern Central African Republic. A railroad from Bangui to N'Djamena in Chad is also under consideration.

The Central African Republic has an extensive road system, totaling about twelve thousand miles. Only sixty miles of this figure are paved highways, but thirty-six hundred miles of roads can be used in all kinds of weather. These all-weather roads link the larger cities of the Republic. The remaining eight thousand miles of roads are laterite-surfaced or

Bus terminals like this one are found in every Central African town that has a hard-surfaced road.

dirt-surfaced roads. They are frequently unusable in the rainy season. Buses connect towns and haul both freight and people. Major routes link Bangui to Bossangoa and Berberati to Nola.

Several international routes pass through the Republic. Two of these lead toward Douala. Roads leading north into Chad start at Bossembélé and Fort Sibut. And international routes also link the Central African Republic to the Sudan.

International air routes, too, link Bangui to other capitals. Bangui, with its central location, is a logical stopping place for travelers going across the continent. So the Republic is trying to increase its international tourist industry.

Air transport is especially important to Central Africans. Towns and cities are scattered in often remote areas. Even places that can be reached by land and water are days apart by any other means but air. Travel by road from Bangui to the north, for example, may take days. But it

takes only a few hours by airplane.

The Mpoko International Airport near Bangui opened in 1967. Other airports of major importance are in Berberati and Bouar. Government-owned Air Bangui and privately owned Air Centrafrique fly from Mpoko Airport to the country's twenty other airfields.

Air transport is too expensive to be used frequently for freight. Only perishable merchandise such as fresh meat or items that are needed in a hurry arrive by plane. Machine parts and lightweight items may be flown into Bangui or other cities. Occasionally, cotton, coffee, peanuts, or rubber are flown from Bangui.

COMMUNICATIONS

Telephone and telegraph services link Bangui to other cities in the Republic. Direct radioteletype and radiotelephone links make rapid communication possible

80

These workers are building a new road just outside Bangui.

with foreign capitals—Brazzaville, Douala, N'Djamena (Chad), and Paris.

Radio Centrafrique broadcasts in both of the Republic's official languages—Sango and French. Broadcasts cover news of the day, public service announcements, and music. Radio Bangui has five stations and broadcasts in five languages, including English and Arabic. There are 46,000 receivers in the Republic. There is one television station in Bangui, but fewer than fifty television sets in the country.

French is the language of the press.

African Land (*Terre Africaine*), published weekly in Bangui by the Ministry of Information, is the voice of MESAN, the nation's only legal political organization. The Ministry also prints *Central African Press* (*Centrafrique Presse*), a daily paper. *Bangui La So* is a privately owned daily paper with a circulation of only five hundred. The *Official Journal of the Republic* (*Journel officiel de la République*) appears semimonthly. Three monthlies are also printed. The French and Soviet news agencies are represented.

Enchantment of Central African Republic

A UNIQUE SAFARI

A group of hunters led by a young boy walks slowly along a forest path. They look anxiously in every direction. Suddenly the boy shouts, "There!" and all the hunters dash forward with their nets. In a few moments they have their specimens—beautiful butterflies. This is a butterfly safari!

The southwest section of the Central African Republic has a large, varied butterfly population. Young Africans who are skillful in butterfly capture are eager to lead "hunters" on safari for a fair price. The best hunting grounds are only a few hours from Bangui, the capital city.

BANGUI

Most tourists in the Central African Republic begin their visit in the city of Bangui, thirteen hundred feet above sea level. Bangui sits just north of the equator, on the north bank of the Ubangi River. The city is surrounded by low hills and wooded savanna. Although the climate is humid, mornings and evenings are cool and pleasant.

Tourists find a wide choice of hotels, restaurants, and entertainment in Bangui. The Rock and the Safari Hotels, both built on the banks of the Ubangi, offer luxury-class accommodations. Downtown, tourists can choose among a number of hotels.

The modern and beautiful Safari Hotel is located in downtown Bangui.

CENTRAL AFRICAN REPUBLIC PHOTOGRAPHIC LIBRARY

A traveler can fly from Bangui to anywhere in the world by way of connecting flights in other major African cities.

The restaurants of Bangui offer French, Portuguese, Indochinese, Caribbean, and Algerian dishes, as well as local menus. On the water's edge, the Rock Hotel has an outdoor restaurant under the shade trees.

Taxis and buses run in Bangui. Automobiles for rent are also available. Fifteen service stations and thirty garages that repair vehicles are located in Bangui.

The city has much to interest visitors and residents alike. There are a bustling market, a busy river port, residential areas of varied architectural styles, artisan centers, and large parks. Frescoes located in the Chamber of Commerce building depict African life. The Boganda Museum focuses on the Republic's history and culture. The African Arts and Crafts Center produces a wide selection of ivory and wood carvings, metal sculpture, musical instruments, and traditional clothing.

Bangui has seven sports stadiums. Spectators can watch bicycle racing or soccer and tennis matches. Private clubs offer water skiing, swimming, flying lessons, judo matches, golf, and riding lessons.

There are several movie theaters, discotheques, and nightclubs with dancing. Bangui-Rock-Club plays the latest music from Paris. In the residential areas, the sounds of traditional drumming and singing can often be heard.

The center of modern Bangui reflects the influence of French colonial days. Wide avenues lined with mango, flame, and palm trees connect shopping centers, government buildings, schools, hospitals, and the homes of foreign residents. Not far from the European center of town is the busy African market. The market is surrounded by covered verandas, where merchants sit to sell their fresh food and local products. Smoked fish, grilled shishkabob, grapefruit, avocados, mangoes, pineapples, or peanuts are sold for people to snack on. Also for sale are cloth, jewelry, and household goods.

Clustered around the commercial and industrial core of the city are residential areas. African residential communities are organized by ethnic groups or by professions. The settlements tend to be dispersed, with open space between the houses. Houses are usually rectangular structures surrounded by verandas and flower gardens. The houses are made out of bamboo, clay, and palm leaves. Wooden panels form the windows and doorways. Often, the exteriors of the homes are elaborately decorated.

The neighborhoods vary in appearance.

Bangui's Palace Hotel was built during colonial times.

Some ethnic groups enclose their houses with bamboo walls. Others plant gardens of corn or bananas around their homes. Interiors, too, reflect the individual tastes of the residents. Furnishings in the Muslim quarter of town are likely to consist of many mats and cushions, perhaps a chair, and a table. Houses in other sections might have more chairs and tables, and often pictures on the walls.

Around 1900 Bangui was only a small village. The simple settlement took its name from the local African word for "rapids," since the nearby rapids on the Ubangi gave rise to the community. Boats could not continue their journey upstream, and their owners had to stop at Bangui to transfer their goods.

Today Bangui is a thriving modern city of more than 250,000 people. It is the main river port, commercial hub, political capital, and industrial center for the Republic's 1.7 million people.

The first push for growth came around 1900, when the French military commander made the settlement his headquarters. Only a few hundred people lived there at that time. By 1940 the population had grown to twenty thousand. Ten years later it was eighty thousand and still growing. Today the population is estimated to be over three times the 1950 figure.

The city has grown so rapidly that it had little time to plan for orderly development. Nevertheless, in 1950, the city government worked out a general development plan. The plan has three basic goals: to maintain separate zones for commerce, industry, and residences; to avoid traffic jams by building a fast-road and a slow-road system; and to fit Bangui into its larger, regional context.

The government has tried to implement this plan. City officials hope to build two circular roads to serve the region. The inner one will link local residential areas. The outer one will link the industrial zone to the port and to routes leading away from the city. Also included in current plans are efforts of regional development. Fruit orchards and small-scale farming located as near as six to twelve miles from the city will improve job opportunities in the urban area. It is also hoped that cattle raising and larger-scale farms can be developed near the city.

AWAY FROM THE CITY

Depending on the direction one goes in, travel away from Bangui leads to rain forest, savanna, or semidesert.

The forest presents a world of shade and light, giant trees, unusual foliage, dense undergrowth, wild game, and colorful birds. The people of the forest live in wooden houses and earn their living by hunting, trading, or lumberjacking.

In the savanna region, there are vast stretches of open plains, blue skies, scattered trees and bushes, farmland, and herds of cattle. Rivers flow quietly through the countryside. The savanna is more densely populated than the forest.

Above and below: Banda dancers from near Bambari perform a traditional dance.

The cloth market at Bangui's Bokassa Market is a fascinating spot to visit.

These rural people live in thatch houses surrounded by tilled fields. They are usually farmers, cattlekeepers, or artisans.

The northern region is a preview of the desert of Chad. Settlements are widely scattered, and some people live a nomadic life, wandering with their animals.

Throughout the Republic, rivers offer the scenic beauty of waterfalls, rapids, cascades, and flowing streams. Parks and reserves protect the variety of wildlife found in the country.

Only an hour's cruise downstream from Bangui along the Ubangi River are the churning rapids of Zinga. A forest road leads from Zinga to the village of M'Baiki, the site of a sawmill and coffee plantations. Nearby is the village of Loko, inhabited by pygmies.

Sixty miles overland, northwest of Bangui, is Boali. On the nearby M'Bali River are spectacular waterfalls that are higher than Niagara Falls. The falls are lighted from December through June. Another waterfall is on the M'Bi river southwest of Bossembélé.

GAME RESERVES AND NATIONAL PARKS

Near N'Dele are several reserves and a national park, each with similar terrain and animal life. The reserves are vast plateaus of forested savanna about 1,500 to 2,800 feet above sea level. Occasionally, granite buttes tower above the plains. Elands, elephants, lions, hyenas, rhinoceroses, and jackals roam the reserves.

With 2,500,000 acres, the Bamingui-Bangoran National Park has been a hunting reserve since 1916. Twenty years later, it became a national park.

Near Birao in the extreme northeastern part of the country are two more national parks. The reserves cover a total of 12,240 square miles. Created in 1916, the National Park of Saint Floris includes 251,750 acres of wooded savanna and is at an altitude of 1,520 feet. Thousands of birds inhabit this park. In the dry season, there are large numbers of elephants, buffalo, antelopes, and hyenas. Lions, giraffes, and rhinoceroses also live there.

The National Park of André Félix is south of Birao. Created in 1960, it encompasses 425,000 acres of wooded savanna at an altitude of 1,520 feet. Its animal and bird populations are similar to those in Saint Floris.

Three other reserves offer special attractions. The Damara-Sibut Reserve, only 60 miles from Bangui, is the home of large elephants. Lobaye-Nola Reserve, 180 miles from Bangui, contains herds of antelope.

The reserves and parks, the geographic regions of the country, the quiet villages, and the bustling capital city offer the tourist a panorama of diverse populations and scenery. This country situated in the middle of Africa offers a glimpse of the natural and human wealth of the entire continent. The enchantment of the Central African Republic is truly the enchantment of Africa.

Handy Reference Section

Political:
Official Name—Central African Republic
   (1977: Central African Empire)
Capital City—Bangui
Monetary Unit—CFA franc
Official Languages—Sango and French
Independence Day—August 13, 1960
National Hero—Barthelemy Boganda
Flag—Four horizontal stripes of blue,
   white, green, and yellow with red ver-
   tical stripe in center and five-pointed
   star in upper-left corner
National Motto—"Unity-Dignity-Work"
National Anthem—*The Rebirth,* by Bar-
   thelemy Boganda

Geographical:
Area—240,535 square miles
Highest Point—4,658 feet (Mount
   Kayagangiri)
Lowest Point—1,340 feet
Greatest Length—475 miles
Greatest Width—900 miles

POPULATION

Population—1,720,000 (1973 esti-
   mate)
Density—4-10 people per square mile
Annual Growth Rate—3 percent
Birth Rate (per 1000)—48
Death Rate (per 1000)—26
Average Life Span—40 years
Primary School Attendance—50 percent
Literacy Rate—10 percent
Urban Literacy Rate—15-25 percent
Per Capita Income—$136

POPULATION OF
PRINCIPAL CITIES (estimated)

Bangui	250,000
Boali	248,000
Bouar	52,000
Berberati	42,000
Bambari	39,000
Bossangoa	38,000
Bangassou	32,000
Bria	29,000
M'Baiki	21,000

HOLIDAYS

Anniversary of Boganda's Death—
March 29
Labor Day—May 1
Government Installation Day—May 15
Anniversary of Boganda's Election to
French National Assembly—November
10
National Day—December 1

ETHNIC GROUPS (percent)

Banda	31
Baya-Mandjia	38
M'Baka	7
Others	24

RELIGIONS (percent)

Animist	60
Christian	35
Muslim	5

MAIN POLITICAL DIVISIONS

Prefecture	*Principal Place*
Bamingui-Bangoran	N'dele
Kemo-Gribingui	Fort Sibut
Lobaye	M'Baiki
Lower Kotto	Mobayé
M'Bomou	Bangassou
Nana-Mamberé	Bouar
Ombella-Mpoko	Boali
Ouaka	Bambari
Ouham	Bossangoa
Ouham-Pendé	Bozoum
Upper M'Bomou	Yakotoko
Upper Kotto	Bria
Upper Sangha	Berberati
Vakaga	Birao

SANGO VOCABULARY

(Note: Some of these phrases show the influence of the French language on Sango.)

Good morning.	Balao.
Goodbye.	Balao.
How are you?	Mon yeke nzoni?
Fine, thank you.	Mereci mingui.
What's your name?	Ere timo a yeke yen?
My name is____.	Iri ti mbi a yeke____.
Come here.	Ga nando so.
Excuse me.	Paradone mbi.
Not at all.	Mbe ke.
yes	hin
no	hin-hin
mother	mama
father	baba

sister	ita ti wali	water	ngou
brother	ita ti kole	today	lasso
friend	songo	tomorrow	kekereke
food	kobe		

YOU HAVE A DATE WITH HISTORY

16th century—Trade networks cross the Republic

17th century—Muslim societies raid Republic as source of slaves: refugees flee to forests and mountains

1800—Zande move to source of Uele River, establish kingdoms

1820s—Baya-Mandjia move in

1830s—Banda move into Republic

by 1870—Muslim merchant-princes establish empires north and east of Republic; slave raids continue

1877—Henry Morton Stanley contacts Boubangui people

1880—Pierre Savorgnan de Brazza makes treaties with Boubangui and other river peoples

1884—Rabah makes N'dele his capital for several years, then moves north into Chad

1889—Michel Dolisie founds Bangui (June 26)

1893—First missionaries arrive in Bangui

1894—French establish post at Berberati; French formally declare formation of Oubangui-Chari (July)

1898—Concessions granted to French companies; French and British troops meet at Fashoda in Sudan (July); French retreat after British threaten war (July)

1899—French and British decide boundary between Sudan and Oubangui-Chari (March 21)

1900—Rabah killed by French in Chad (April 22)

1903—Revolts break out in Baya-Mandjia areas

1906—Oubangui-Chari and Chad become one colony

1910—French Equatorial Africa formed; Barthelemy Boganda born in Lobaye (April 4)

1912—Senoussi defeated by French

1920—Chad becomes separate territory

1921—Jean-Bedel Bokassa born in Lobaye (February 22)

1927—Baya of Haute Sangha rebel against French because of forced labor for railroad construction

1931—Baya-Mandjia revolt crushed; railroad completed

1938—Boganda ordained to Roman Catholic priesthood (March 17)

1939—Bokassa joins French army

1944—Brazzaville Conference convenes and reaffirms policies of Governor Eboué (January)

1946—French Union created

1948—Boganda founds Cooperative

Society of Lobaye-Lesse

1951—Boganda called upon to settle dispute between Lobaye Cooperative and Portuguese (January 10); Boganda sentenced to jail (March 29)

1954—Riot breaks out in Berberati (April 30); Boganda disperses crowd (May 1)

1956—Boganda elected to territorial assembly (January); French pass *loi cadre* (enabling act) (June)

1957—Boganda becomes president of Grand Council of French Equatorial Africa (June)

1958—Referendum held, Republic votes to join French Community (September)

1959—Republic adopts first constitution; Boganda dies (March 29); David Dacko becomes president (April 30)

1960—New constitution adopted; Goumba founds MEDAC as rival to Dacko's regime (June); transfer of sovereignty signed (July 12); full independence declared (August 13); Republic joins United Nations; MEDAC demonstrates against Dacko (November)

1962—Goumba sentenced to life imprisonment; MESAN revived as mass party (July)

1963—Bokassa becomes army's chief of staff; Republic joins World Bank and International Monetary Fund

1964—Constitution rewritten to stress MESAN's role; Customs Union of Central African States (UDEAC) formed (December 8)

1965—Common African and Malagasy Union (OCAM) formed (February); Dacko announces new budget that requires 10 percent reduction in salaries (December); Bokassa seizes power, deposes Dacko (December 31)

1966—Bokassa declares new regime, sets up Revolutionary Council; Parliament dissolved

1967—Bokassa takes over Ministry of the Interior and secretary general of MESAN; Customs Union of Central African States expanded (December)

1968—Republic joins Union of Central African States (UEAC)

1969—Bokassa accuses Banza of plotting coup d'état, has him executed

1970—University of Jean-Bedel Bokassa opens in Bangui (February)

1971—Bokassa enlarges Republic's army; OCAM becomes Afro-Malagasy-Mauritanian Common Organization

1972—Bokassa becomes "President for Life" (March)

1973—Bokassa accuses M'Bongo of plotting coup d'etat, imprisons him; Boganda takes over ministries (April); Republic breaks diplomatic ties with Israel (October 21)

1974—Bokassa becomes field marshal (May 20); Bokassa enlarges personal power in government council (June); customs union moves headquarters to Bangui (August 12)

1977—Bokassa changes name of country to Central African Empire, proclaims himself emperor

Index

About the Authors

With the publication of his first book for school use when he was twenty, **Allan Carpenter** began a career as an author that has spanned more than 135 books—with more still to be published in the Enchantment of Africa series for Childrens Press. After teaching in the public schools of Des Moines, Mr. Carpenter began his career as an educational publisher at the age of twenty-one when he founded the magazine *Teachers Digest*. In the field of educational periodicals, he was responsible for many innovations. During his many years in publishing, he has perfected a highly organized approach to handling large volumes of factual material: after extensive traveling and having collected all possible materials, he systematically reviews and organizes everything. From his apartment high in Chicago's John Hancock Building, Allan recalls: "My collection and assimilation of materials on the states and countries began before the publication of my first book." Allan is the founder of Carpenter Publishing House and of Infordata International, Inc., publishers of *Issues in Education* and *Index to U.S. Government Periodicals*. When he is not writing or traveling, his principal avocation is music. He has been the principal bassist of many symphonies, and he managed the country's leading non-professional symphony for twenty-five years.

Janice E. Baker spent two fascinating years as a Peace Corps teacher in Guinea. During that time, she not only came to know well the people of Guinea, but also had the opportunity to travel all over West Africa, discovering first-hand much about the other countries and peoples of this part of the continent. Her interest in African culture and history prompted her to continue her formal education in this field. In 1971 she received both a master's degree in Comparative World History (Africa) and a Certificate in African Studies from the University of Wisconsin.

T. 7

967	CARPENTER
C	
	Central African republic

DATE DUE	BORROWER'S NAME	ROOM NO.
MAR 1 8 1980	R. Frazier	22
MAR 1 7 1981	Henry Okonma	41
MAR 1 8 1982	Riehl	
OCT 2 5 1982		

967	CARPENTER
C	
	Central African republic